Differentiated Instructional Strategies Professional Learning Guide

Differentiated Instructional Strategies Professional Learning Guide

One Size Doesn't Fit All

Third Edition

Gayle H. Gregory

CORWIN
A SAGE Company

CORWIN
A SAGE Company

FOR INFORMATION:

Corwin

A SAGE Company

2455 Teller Road

Thousand Oaks, California 91320

(800) 233-9936

www.corwin.com

SAGE Publications Ltd.

1 Oliver's Yard

55 City Road

London EC1Y 1SP

United Kingdom

SAGE Publications India Pvt. Ltd.

B 1/I 1 Mohan Cooperative Industrial Area

Mathura Road, New Delhi 110 044

India

SAGE Publications Asia-Pacific Pte. Ltd.

3 Church Street

#10-04 Samsung Hub

Singapore 049483

Acquisitions Editor: Jessica Allan

Editorial Assistant: Heidi Arndt

Production Editor: Laura Barrett

Copy Editor: Sarah J. Duffy

Typesetter: C&M Digitals (P) Ltd.

Proofreader: Joyce Li

Indexer: Judy Hunt

Cover Designer: Candace Harman

Permissions Editor: Karen Ehrmann

Copyright © 2013 by Corwin

A catalog record of this book is available from the Library of Congress.

ISBN 978-1-4522-9164-2

13 14 15 16 17 10 9 8 7 6 5 4 3 2 1

Contents

Acknowledgments

I am indebted to many professional educators for their work, writings, and examples. Those whose influence can be seen in this book include Pat Wolfe, Howard Gardner, Daniel Goleman, David Sousa, Bob Sylwester, Eric Jensen, Tony Gregorc, Bernice McCarthy, Carol Rolheiser, Bob Marzano, Jay McTighe, Carol Ann Tomlinson, Carol O'Connor, Pam Robbins, Robin Fogarty, and Kay Burke, to mention a few. Special thanks go to friend and colleague Joanne Quinn for her ongoing enthusiasm and support.

I thank my family members for their love and support and offer special thanks to my husband, Joe, for his understanding, encouragement, and ideas during the long hours of writing, listening, and editing.

About the Author

 **Gayle H. Gregory** has been a teacher in elementary, middle, and secondary schools. For many years, she taught in schools with extended periods of instructional time (block schedules). She has had extensive districtwide experience as a curriculum consultant and staff development coordinator. She was course director at York University for the Faculty of Education, teaching in the teacher education program. She now consults internationally (Europe, Asia, North and South America, Australia) with teachers, administrators, and staff developers in the areas of managing change, differentiated instruction, brain-compatible learning, block scheduling, emotional intelligence, instructional and assessment practices, cooperative group learning, presentation skills, renewal of secondary schools, enhancing teacher quality, and coaching and mentoring.

Gayle is the coauthor of *Teacher Teams That Get Results*; *Designing Brain-Compatible Learning*; *Differentiated Instructional Strategies: One Size Doesn't Fit All, Second Edition*; *Designing Brain-Compatible Learning, Third Edition*; *Differentiating Instruction With Style: Aligning Teacher and Learner Intelligences for Maximum Achievement*; *Differentiated Literacy Strategies for Student Growth and Achievement in Grades 7–12*; *Differentiated Literacy Strategies for Student Growth and Achievement in Grades K–6*; *Data Driven Differentiation in the Standards-Based Classroom*; *Differentiated Instructional Strategies in Practice: Training, Implementation, and Supervision*; and *Thinking Inside the Block Schedule: Strategies for Teaching in Extended Periods of Time*. She has been featured in *Video Journal of Education*'s best-selling elementary and secondary videos *Differentiating Instruction to Meet the Needs of All Learners*.

Gayle is committed to lifelong learning and professional growth for herself and others. She may be contacted by e-mail at gregorygayle@netscape.net. Her Web site is www.gaylehgregory.com.

Introduction

ADULTS NEED DIFFERENTIATED LEARNING OPPORTUNITIES, TOO ■

This book is intended to assist school administrators and staff developers in strengthening the concept of differentiated instruction in schools and classrooms to better meet the individual and diverse needs of students.

It is apparent to many of us who provide professional development for teachers that adults need differentiated learning opportunities just as children do because adults begin at different places based on their backgrounds, experiences, abilities, and interests. Thus, this book covers the basic elements of differentiated instruction as well as how teachers and staff developers as a professional learning community can focus on those principles.

Part I highlights the attributes and research of quality staff development and job-embedded training strategies, including book study, video and popcorn sessions, and action research.

Part II offers a chapter-by-chapter series of activities and discussion starters based on the book *Differentiated Instructional Strategies: One Size Doesn't Fit All*, 3rd ed. (Gregory & Chapman, 2013) that will facilitate training with a book study group or as individual activities at faculty meetings.

Part III examines teacher approaches to change, using familiar tools such as the Concerns-Based Adoption Model (Hord, Rutherford, Huling-Austin, & Hall, 1987) and adopter types (Rogers, 1995) ranging from Innovators to Resistors. Coaching and supervision using observation tools for the differentiated classroom are covered, and an implementation profile is offered to assess where members of the learning community are in the process of adapting to differentiated instructional strategies.

PART I

Building School Capacity Through Professional Development

I-1

School Capacity and Student Achievement

Educational policies and programs for professional development should support school capacity for change and improvement, according to Newmann, King, and Youngs (2000). School improvement and capacity for change are dependent on multiple factors:

- Teachers' knowledge, skills, and dispositions, thus quality staff development
- Professional learning communities, thus collaborative learning
- Program coherence, thus consensus and focus
- Technical resources, thus materials and training
- Principal leadership, thus support and encouragement

All of these elements are necessary for improving the quality of instruction, curriculum, and assessment in order to increase student achievement. Principals and teacher leaders who want to improve conditions that build school capacity must focus on these components, evaluating evidence of them in their schools as they develop learning organizations that can manage and sustain change (see Figure 1).

Figure 1   Influences on school capacity and student achievement

Supportive School Culture

Quality Staff Development in a
Professional Learning Community

Teacher's Sense of
Competence and Confidence

**Student
Achievement**

Teacher's Sense of
Competence and Confidence

Quality Staff Development in a
Professional Learning Community

Supportive School Culture

■ ESSENTIAL ELEMENTS FOR BUILDING SCHOOL CAPACITY FOR CHANGE

Student Achievement. At the heart of school improvement is student achievement. Everything we do in schools should be focused on increasing students' knowledge and skills.

Teachers' Sense of Competence and Confidence. Teachers who are not valued and respected often do not feel comfortable or empowered enough to make the changes necessary to improve student learning. Those teachers who feel that they are incapable or lack the skills to differentiate instruction need continual support, encouragement, and reinforcement of their efforts so that they have the will and skill to succeed in differentiating instruction.

Quality Staff Development in a Professional Learning Community and a Supportive School Culture. A teacher's sense of efficacy (Guskey, 1994) is what a teacher believes he or she can do to effect student learning. Thus the same safe, supportive climate that we want in the classroom for students must also be created for the adult learners in the school community. People who enjoy their work and find their workplace pleasant, nonthreatening, yet challenging usually feel more confident than those who don't.

They are able to take the risks involved in order to learn and develop new skills and strategies.

"Emotional hijacking" (Goleman, 1995), which causes people to react emotionally to stress, threat, or fatigue, makes them feel helpless and unable to think rationally. That is not what we want for learners, whether they are age 5 or age 45. Adults in a state of relaxed alertness are more confident and more open to new learning and change, just as their students are. Treating adult learners with the same respect that we want for our students only models good practice. People who feel valued and are in a state of relaxed alertness are more likely to take risks and venture into new and challenging areas of instruction and assessment.

POWERFUL STAFF DEVELOPMENT SUPPORTS CHANGE AND INNOVATION

Professional Development is about change—change in what you know and believe about teaching and learning and in what you can do in the classroom. Part of bringing about real change is creating a context or climate in which change is less difficult.

—David Collins (1998)

In *A New Vision for Staff Development*, Sparks and Hirsh (1997) point out that powerful staff development supports innovation, experimentation, and collegial sharing. Staff development has real impact when it engages people in daily planning, critiquing, and problem solving, and when it provides ongoing practice-based assistance. Powerful staff development deepens the content knowledge, instructional skills, and assessment skills that help teachers regularly monitor student learning.

Powerful professional development is also *results-driven* staff development, connected to what students need to know and be able to do. It provides educators with the knowledge and skills they need to ensure student success related to targeted standards, competencies, and expectations.

The content of staff development sessions should be focused on the body of knowledge and skills necessary to produce greater success for students, recognizing that adults need to learn in ways that are comfortable and engaging for them. The school and its organizational structures should support adult learning within the context of the professional learning community.

PROFESSIONAL LEARNING COMMUNITIES

The most promising strategy for sustained, substantive school improvement is developing the ability of school personnel to function as professional learning communities.

—Richard DuFour and Robert Eaker (1998)

Professional learning communities change the climate and purpose of professional dialogue between and among teachers. Dialogue differs from discussion because dialogue increases the depth of understanding of ideas and concepts.

These are the purposes of a professional learning community (Murphy & Lick, 2001):

- Developing a deeper understanding of academic content
- Supporting the implementation of curricula and instructional initiatives
- Identifying a focus for the school's instructional process
- Studying research on teaching and learning
- Monitoring the impact of instructional initiatives on students
- Examining student work

Administrators who want to cultivate professional learning communities within their schools can use the following checklist (adapted from Collins, 1998) to identify activities that cultivate and sustain a professional learning community.

Creating and Sustaining a Professional Learning Community

____ Do teachers talk regularly about teaching and learning?

____ Do teachers have opportunities to observe each other teach?

____ Do teachers examine student work and solve problems collaboratively about the next steps in the learning process?

____ Are there opportunities for book studies or action research facilitated by teachers or administrators?

____ Do teachers have shared planning time to develop lessons and share strategies during the school day?

____ Do teachers have time to examine data to determine how students are progressing?

____ Are there opportunities to play as well as work together?

____ Do people give advice as well as ask for suggestions?

____ Do teachers share and support one another's efforts?

____ Are training and developing new skills and knowledge collegial experiences in which teachers can share a common language, implement together, and coach one another?

____ Do teachers participate in setting the school's focus for differentiation?

____ Is collective decision making part of the process of designing staff development?

In the words of Peter Senge (1990),

We can then build . . . organizations where people continuously expand their capacity to create the results they truly desire, where new and expansive patterns of thinking are nurtured, where collective aspiration is set free, and where people are continually learning how to learn together. (p. 3)

School Culture

The culture of an enterprise plays the dominant role in exemplary performance.

—Terrence E. Deal and Kent D. Peterson (1999)

The culture of the school facilitates or inhibits its evolution into a professional learning organization. Deal and Peterson (1999) suggest that culture includes a shared mission and purpose within which people work, and it includes the norms, values, and beliefs that make up the fabric of the school.

The school's mission and purpose come from the values, beliefs, assumptions, and norms embraced by its faculty. *Values* are what the organization stands for, that which gives the work a deeper meaning. *Beliefs* are what we understand and believe as truth. *Assumptions* are created through dialogue that facilitates shared values and beliefs. *Norms* are those stated or unstated group behaviors that all members expect to be upheld in their interactions.

These are examples of positive norms:

- Everyone's ideas are respected.
- Everyone has a voice and an opinion.
- Everyone is positive in talking about the school and students.
- Everyone is entitled to support and help.

These are examples of negative norms:

- Put down rather than put up.
- Pretend to be involved.
- Criticism and complaints are okay.
- Negative leaders are powerful.

Principals and staff developers must take every opportunity to create dialogue that will lead teachers toward a more positive school culture in which shared vision and mission can prevail and influence actions.

LEARNING AND IMPLEMENTATION ◼

Joyce and Showers (1995) reported that the levels of transfer increase based on the type of learning experiences and training in which people are involved. Being exposed only to theory and modeling results in very little actual application in the classroom, whereas those teachers who have opportunities to practice in risk-free conditions increase their skill level considerably. Further, teachers who are in collaborative situations with a coaching component that includes study teams and opportunities to problem-solve with supportive colleagues have an 80%–90% better chance of applying the innovation in their classroom repertoire, thus the power of job-embedded learning.

Figure 2 displays the percentages of awareness, skill attainment, and application that can be expected from the following components of staff development training:

- Presentation of theory
- Modeling of the innovation
- Practice and low-risk feedback
- Coaching, study teams, and peer interaction

Note that in-service training, workshops, and how-to-do-its are all useful and important in the change process, as is the opportunity to practice in safe environments, but most profound of all is the necessity for ongoing dialogue with coaches, peers, and study teams. Sharing, problem solving, and collaborative supports are essential to facilitating implementation and transfer into the classroom and into a teacher's repertoire.

Figure 2   Training, implementation, and transfer to teacher's repertoire

Components of Training	Awareness Plus Concept Understanding	Skill Attainment	Application/Problem Solving
Presentation of theory	85%	15%	5%–10%
Modeling of the innovation	85%	15%	5%–10%
Practice and low-risk feedback	85%	80%	10%–15%
Coaching, study teams, and peer interaction	90%	90%	80%–90%

SOURCE: Adapted from Joyce & Showers (1995).

I-2

Job-Embedded Strategies for Differentiated Professional Development

It is now recognized that learning within the schoolhouse during working hours is a powerful experience for educators. To sustain a professional learning community, this job-embedded learning must be an ongoing activity. Some of the purposes served by job-embedded staff development include the following:

- Developing a deeper understanding of content and increasing teachers' knowledge base
- Supporting implementation of curricular, instructional, and assessment initiatives
- Providing coherence and focus to school growth and improvement
- Focusing on a specific, targeted schoolwide need
- Continuing the professional dialogue about teaching and learning

Strategies for accomplishing job-embedded staff development include the following:

- Study groups
- Coaching
- Cadres

- Video viewing
- Journaling
- Jigsaw strategy
- Action research
- Portfolios
- Curriculum development
- Examining student work
- Mentoring
- Cases

Any of these job-embedded learnings should focus on increasing student achievement through deeper understanding of academic content and increased instructional initiatives. These learnings should support school-wide needs and continue the study of teaching and learning while monitoring their impact. Time for collegial dialogue is always an essential component of job-embedded staff development. Some of the most effective job-embedded strategies that can be used to explore differentiated instruction include study groups, video viewing, the jigsaw strategy, action research, and teacher inquiry (see also Easton, 2004).

■ STUDY GROUPS

What Are Study Groups?

Study groups are opportunities to dialogue around meaningful information about teaching and learning. In dialogue, the goal is deeper meaning and understanding. It focuses on inquiry, reflection, and exploration. A journal article or a book chapter about teacher needs that support student learning may be selected as a focus of the group. Part II of this volume provides guidelines for using *Differentiated Instructional Strategies: One Size Doesn't Fit All* (3rd ed.; Gregory & Chapman, 2013) as such a focus.

Why Participate in Study Groups?

Teachers in study groups get a chance to peruse research and current information about teaching and learning. They are able to explore effective instructional strategies and other resources. Teachers may examine new skills and dialogue around their use in the classrooms with students. During a study group session, teachers may also set goals and create plans for implementation.

How Do We Facilitate a Study Group?

1. Select a book chapter or journal article that may be preread or perhaps organized as a jigsaw (see Jigsaw Strategy, later in the chapter) during the study group session. Many teachers don't have time to read prior to the session, and a jigsaw facilitates learning when prereading is impossible.

2. Appoint someone to prepare an advance organizer to help focus discussion and to record key ideas (Figure 3).

Figure 3 Advance organizer for study group

An idea that interested me	How it was used	How I could use it	Notes
An idea that interested me			
An idea that interested me			
An idea that interested me			

3. Assign roles to each member of the group. Roles may include Recorder, Questioner, Clarifier, Encourager, Timekeeper, Facilitator, and Summarizer. Figure 4 offers helpful language that group members can use as they fill each of these roles.

4. Develop questions that ensure that dialogue is focused and purposeful. Encourage all members of the group to pose questions for dialogue that would interest and benefit themselves and others.

5. Ask group members to set goals and predict the impact of trying some of the ideas or commit to further exploration of the ideas discovered.

6. Ask group members to incorporate journaling and reflective organizers as they explore some of the ideas from the study group in their classroom practice. A focus from the study group can often lead to action research to investigate the impact of a particular technique or strategy in greater depth.

■ POPCORN AND A VIDEO

What Is Video Viewing?

Videos provide an opportunity for teachers to view classrooms in action and to hear and see new research and innovative processes that can be used in their own classrooms and schools. It has been said that a picture is worth a thousand words. Seeing techniques used by real teachers with real students is exciting and breeds confidence in other teachers. Some videos may also provide research and background information from experts and master teachers.

Why View Videos?

Videos are a powerful way to spark discussion about teaching and learning and actually see teachers working in classrooms with students. Teachers do not often have a chance to observe other teachers or to analyze and/or critique the teaching process. Videos give them an opportunity to question the rationale behind the instructional and assessment processes that teachers select. They bring each strategy to life and let teachers see other teachers using it successfully. They also illustrate student behavior with a particular strategy or technique and provide a way of seeing and hearing experts share research and innovations that merit consideration.

How Do We Facilitate Video Viewing?

1. Prepare an advance organizer to collect key issues or information. See Figure 5 for a sample that uses de Bono's (1987) Thinking CorT strategies Plus, Minus, and Interesting, or Figure 6 for the Six Lenses for Examination method adapted from de Bono's (1999) *Six Thinking Hats.*

2. View the video.

3. Facilitate the dialogue following the video viewing. If participants used Plus-Minus-Interesting (Figure 5) or Six Lenses for Examination (Figure 6), those headings can be used to organize the dialogue.

Figure 4 Bookmarks may be given to people in study groups so that they have helpful language to use when performing their roles (adapted from Robbins, Gregory, & Herndon, 2000)

Encourager

Helpful language:

Great idea.
Thanks for sharing.
What do you think?
Fine idea.
Right on . . . what else . . . ?
Thank you . . . .

Questioner

Helpful language:

Who could . . . ?
What's a first step?
How could we . . . ?
What's the best plan?
When can we . . . ?
Any ideas . . . ?

Clarifier

Helpful language:

Is this what . . . ?
Explain to me
Say again . . . .
Did I hear . . . ?
I think you said . . . .
It sounds to me . . . .

Summarizer

Helpful language:

I think we agree that . . . .
Most of us said . . . .
Some of us . . . .
Others differ . . . .
It seems to me . . . .
In summary . . . .

Recorder

Helpful language:

Perhaps . . . .
I think . . . .
My idea . . . .
Suppose . . . .
Another idea . . . .
Anyone else . . . .

Facilitator

Helpful language:

Whose turn is it?
Has everyone given an idea?
We have ____ minutes.
That's three done, we have ____
    more to do.
What do you think?
Are we ready to move on?

Figure 5   Advance organizer for video viewing

Plus: What are the positives that you noticed?		How could you use this?
Minus: What do you have concerns about or do not agree with?		What would you do differently?
Interesting: What did you find insightful or intriguing?		Next steps for you . . .

SOURCE: Adapted from de Bono (1987).

Figure 6   Six lenses for examination

Viewers select one lens to use as they view the video, and they bring that information to the dialogue that follows the viewing.

Clear Lens: What are the facts?
Red Lens: What feelings do these ideas evoke?
Blue Lens: What reflections might you have?
Cloudy Lens: What might be the downside of these ideas?
Green Lens: What are the creative possibilities that may be explored?
Yellow Lens: What are the positives that may be involved?

Clear lens	What are the facts?	
Red lens	What feelings do these ideas evoke?	
Blue lens	What reflections might you have?	
Cloudy lens	What might be the downside of these ideas?	
Green lens	What are the creative possibilities that may be explored?	
Yellow lens	What are the positives that may be involved?	

SOURCE: Adapted from de Bono (1999).

Other advance organizers can also provide the framework for discussion.

4. Consider possible applications and ideas.

5. As a group, decide on the next steps, such as reading an article, viewing another video, trying an idea, or attending a workshop or conference.

6. Arrange a follow-up meeting time.

7. Suggest that viewers also record their personal reflections (Figure 7).

■ JIGSAW STRATEGY

What Is Jigsaw?

The jigsaw is a way to read a journal article or book chapter, view a video, or learn new information interdependently with a small group of colleagues.

Why Use Jigsaw?

The jigsaw strategy (Aronson, 1978; Slavin, 1994) is a useful way for staff to learn or explore new information in a way that encourages dialogue and fosters interdependence among faculty as they discuss implications of

Figure 7   Personal reflection journal jigsaw strategy

One idea that interests me is . . .	Something I'd like to try is . . .
One step I can take tomorrow is . . .	I wonder . . .

new innovations or research for their classrooms. It also helps with fostering a more inclusive culture as teachers depend on others for their contributions to complete the group's thinking.

How Do We Facilitate the Jigsaw Strategy?

1. Find two or three journal articles or one article with enough information to divide into three or four sections.

2. Divide the staff into base groups of three to five members, depending on the number of articles or sections to be read.

3. Assign each staff member in the base group a section to read (10 to 15 minutes of independent reading).

4. Have people who have read the same section form small expert groups to discuss key aspects or issues from their article (15 to 20 minutes).

5. Have experts return to their base groups, and invite each person to share the key points from their reading and discussion with the other members of the group (20 to 30 minutes), using an advance organizer to jot down information that is important to them and their work (Figures 8 and 9).

6. Facilitate a large-group discussion identifying implications of this information for students and the school.

7. Make some decisions about the next steps for training and implementation.

ACTION RESEARCH ■

What Is Action Research?

Like younger learners, teachers have burning questions that they are curious about. As its name implies, action research is a way to use research and inquiry actively in teachers' daily work in classrooms and schools.

Why Do Action Research?

Action research gives teachers an opportunity to investigate subjects that are near and dear to the heart, to pursue personal interests or quests related to teaching and learning.

How Do We Facilitate Action Research?

1. A teacher (or teachers) creates a question relevant to their students and their classroom concerning differentiation. Here are some sample questions:

   • Does a positive climate really make a difference for learners?
   • Do pre-assessment data influence my planning and result in adjustable assignments?

Figure 8   Advance organizer for jigsaw

1. Article or section _____	Ideas/Reactions
	Aha's
2. Article or section _____	Ideas/Reactions
	Aha's
3. Article or section _____	Ideas/Reactions
	Aha's
4. Article or section _____	Ideas/Reactions
	Aha's

Figure 9   Jigsaw strategy for enhancing interdependence among expert
learners

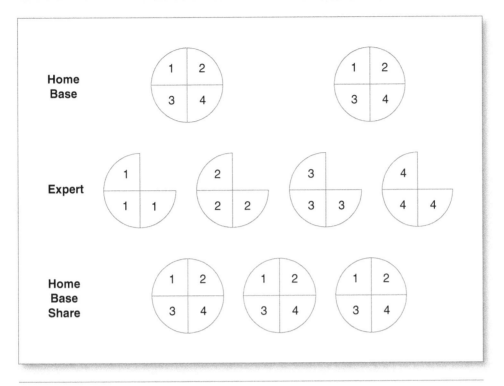

2. A research plan of action is created. This plan should address the
    following questions:

    - How will I establish a baseline?
    - What data will be collected?
    - How will the data be collected? By whom? When?
    - How will the data be analyzed? By whom? When?
    - How will the findings be shared?

3. Individually or collaboratively with colleagues, the teacher refines
    the research question and plan.

4. The research is conducted according to the plan outlined in Step 3.
    Teachers may want to use a time and task agenda (Figure 10), a
    reflective journal, or a double-duty log (Figure 11) to record informa-
    tion and reflections.

5. The teacher analyzes the data and shares the findings with col-
    leagues, using a report, presentation, or other method. Richard
    Sagor's (1992) *How to Conduct Collaborative Action Research* pro-
    vides a detailed discussion of this model for facilitating action
    research. Teachers may also find the Basic Inquiry Model flow
    chart (Figure 12) useful for working through the inquiry process.

Figure 10   Personal agenda to keep track of time and tasks

✳✳✳ A Personal Agenda ✳✳✳

My agenda (name): _____

Beginning on (date): _____

Dates	Student Tasks	How I Used My Time	Reflections	Completion Date, Teacher and Student Sign-Off

Figure 11 Double-duty log

Double-duty logs allow students to record or list facts and information about content or process and then reflect on that information immediately or at another time to integrate it into their thinking and deepen their understanding. It allows students to process the information and make sense or meaning. It also facilitates revisiting the material to clarify or add to the thinking.

Facts or Ideas	Thoughts and Reflections

Figure 12   Flow chart for a basic inquiry model for action research

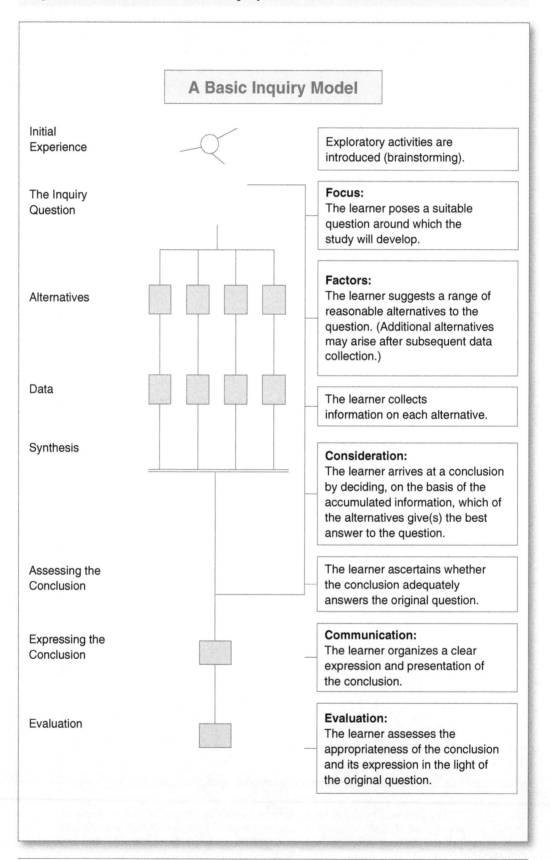

A Basic Inquiry Model

Initial
Experience

> Exploratory activities are
> introduced (brainstorming).

The Inquiry
Question

> **Focus:**
> The learner poses a suitable
> question around which the
> study will develop.

Alternatives

> **Factors:**
> The learner suggests a range of
> reasonable alternatives to the
> question. (Additional alternatives
> may arise after subsequent data
> collection.)

Data

> The learner collects
> information on each alternative.

Synthesis

> **Consideration:**
> The learner arrives at a conclusion
> by deciding, on the basis of the
> accumulated information, which of
> the alternatives give(s) the best
> answer to the question.

Assessing the
Conclusion

> The learner ascertains whether
> the conclusion adequately
> answers the original question.

Expressing the
Conclusion

> **Communication:**
> The learner organizes a clear
> expression and presentation of
> the conclusion.

Evaluation

> **Evaluation:**
> The learner assesses the
> appropriateness of the conclusion
> and its expression in the light of
> the original question.

SOURCE: Ministry of Education (1979, p. 20).

BAGEL BREAKFAST ■

A wonderful administrator in Clark County (Las Vegas), Nevada, invites staff to a bagel breakfast every Tuesday morning. There is always a focus or theme for the breakfast. Sometimes it is an instructional strategy, guest speaker, video viewing, problem solving, article discussion, or minipresentation from a staff member. Anyone may attend, including parents.

One Tuesday I was fortunate enough to attend. Beth had been using one of my books for book study, and she asked if I would do a minisession on graphic organizers. We focused on three: the Venn diagram, the matrix, and the mind map.

Beth challenged teachers to think of a way to use one of those organizers on that day while it was fresh in their minds. As I visited classrooms throughout the day, I was excited to see the kindergarten children with hula hoops comparing and contrasting and first-grade students using a matrix for character, plot, and setting for story writing. Sixth graders were creating mind maps to show the interesting aspects of Nevada. At the next meeting, teachers brought examples of student work that used graphic organizers and discussed their use and their students' learnings.

This principal never missed a chance to help teachers stretch their thinking and get better at their craft. Any principal or teacher leader can also use this strategy at different times of day, for example, Wednesday for lunch or tea after class. Figure 13 offers a reflection piece that may be used for metacognition after one of these sessions.

Figure 13   Shaping up a review

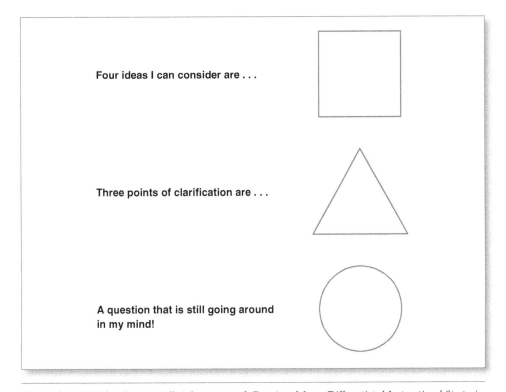

Four ideas I can consider are . . .

Three points of clarification are . . .

A question that is still going around in my mind!

PART II

Book Study Using *Differentiated Instructional Strategies: One Size Doesn't Fit All*, Third Edition, and Other Training Resources

II-1

One Size
Doesn't Fit All

DIFFERENTIATED INSTRUCTION: CONCEPT CLARIFICATION ■

To begin, let's consider the definition of *differentiation* and how to promote that shared vision between and among faculty. Differentiation is a philosophy that enables teachers to plan strategically in order to meet the needs of the diverse learners in classrooms today. Differentiation is not just a set of instructional tools but a philosophy that a teacher and a professional learning community embrace to reach the unique needs of every learner. Prior to reading *Differentiated Instructional Strategies: One Size Doesn't Fit All* (3rd ed.; Gregory & Chapman, 2013) or embarking on the journey of differentiated instruction, invite teachers to participate in a Four Corners activity using Figure 14.

Four Corners

Each teacher takes a few minutes to finish the prompts in each quadrant of the Four Corners form. Then they are invited to walk about the room sharing their ideas with other teachers. This helps teachers open mental files and develop a shared language about differentiation.

Four Corners also serves as a pre-assessment so that the levels of understanding, commitment, and current practices as well as the needs of teachers are evident. This pre-assessment strategy can also be used with students to find out what they already know about a topic, what they are interested in, and which concepts are clear or are still in need of clarification. Four Corners also promotes dialogue and interaction

Figure 14   Four Corners

I think it is . . . I think it's important because . . .	A symbol for it might be . . .
I already meet the needs of my students by . . .	I need to know . . .

among learners and can be used as a focus activity at the beginning of a new topic or as a review before a test.

Brainstorming Options

Following Four Corners, teachers may participate in a brainstorming session using Figure 15 to identify the basic concepts of differentiated instruction and to identify their options for differentiation.

Faculty Meetings as Professional Learning Communities

Often faculty meetings are just a litany of information and paper pushing and have very little to do with professional learning and student achievement. Taking just the first 20 minutes of a faculty meeting to focus on differentiation serves to keep teachers' eyes on the target, to emphasize the coherence of the initiative, to support the process, and to provide resources for implementation.

The strategies that follow may be used for a book study group or individually as staff meeting activities to keep the focus and to support implementation. Most of the training strategies are based on the book *Differentiated Instructional Strategies: One Size Doesn't Fit All* (3rd ed.; Gregory & Chapman, 2013), and the text that follows contains cross-references in parentheses to the relevant pages in that book.

Figure 15   Options for Differentiated Instruction

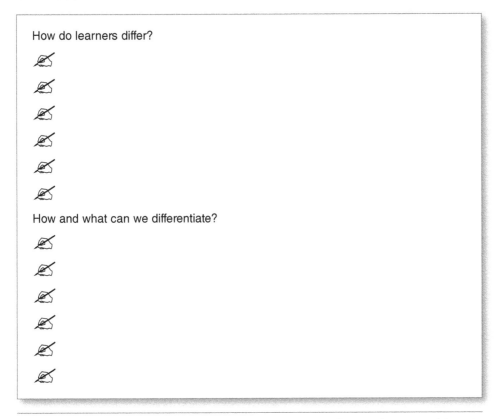

How do learners differ?

How and what can we differentiate?

Book study is an excellent job-embedded training strategy that facilitates dialogue and helps build a professional learning community. Video viewing is also an important training strategy, and some of the activities that follow refer to video training resources by Tomlinson (1998b) and by Gregory and Chapman (2002a, 2002b).

WHY DIFFERENTIATION? (PAGES 5–6) ■

Using Graphic Organizers to Connect Concepts

After reading Chapter 1 ("One Size Doesn't Fit All"), teachers may work in small groups to create a word web with differentiation as the central theme (Figure 16). Word webs are graphic organizers that are verbal or linguistic in nature. Word webs place the concept in the center of the web as a theme, and elements related to the concept branch out from the center.

Mind maps differ from word webs in that they use words and symbolic visual representation rather than words alone. They are useful in demonstrating understanding of a concept and visually depicting a complete

Figure 16   Word webs can be used to organize data, demonstrate understanding of major concepts, and make connections between concepts (Gregory & Parry, 2006).

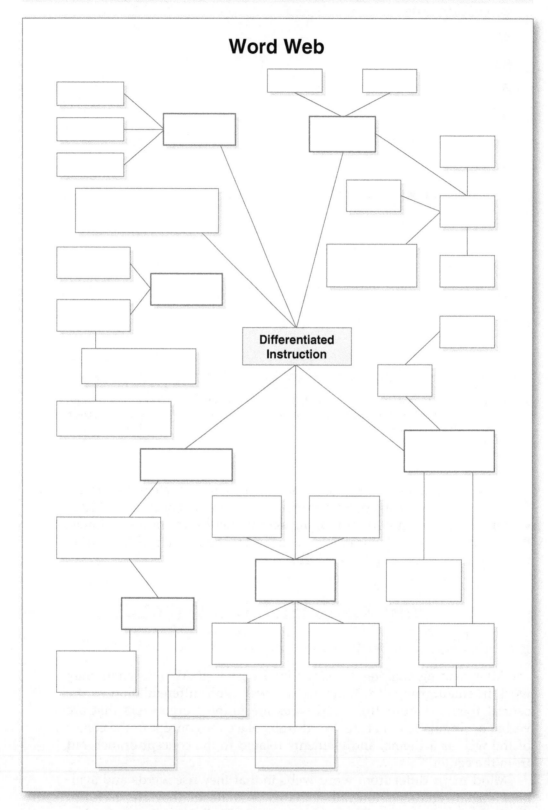

connection of ideas and elements. An alternative strategy to creating a word web would be to ask teachers to use Figure 17 to create a mind map that depicts the attributes of a differentiated classroom and describes what it looks like, sounds like, and feels like.

Collegial Problem Solving During Implementation

It is helpful for teachers to identify their concerns about differentiation so that they can be responded to appropriately. The following strategy may be used to help teachers voice their concerns in a safe environment and also to open up problem-solving dialogue and encourage collegial support during implementation.

Three-Step Problem Solution Seeking

- In supportive groups of three, ask teachers to letter off A, B, and C.
- As Step 1, Person A will share a concern or problem that is related to differentiated instruction.
- As Step 2, Person B will question and clarify the problem and then brainstorm possibilities for solving the situation.
- As Step 3, Person C will listen and record all the ideas and perhaps suggest one that he or she thinks shows promise.
- Ultimately, Person A will decide on the one suggestion that might work for them and describe how they might utilize it (adapted from Bennett, Rolheiser-Bennett, & Stevahn, 1991).

The roles can be rotated within the group so that everyone gets a chance to have his or her problem solved and everyone can help suggest solutions to others in the group. This strategy reinforces the "collective wisdom" housed in each faculty and also strengthens collegial bonds of support that foster a professional learning community.

PLANNING FOR DIFFERENTIATED ■ INSTRUCTION (PAGES 8–10)

Using the Framework

Present the six-column framework for differentiated instruction in Figure 18, suggesting that if we are trying to understand and create classrooms in which differentiated instruction can flourish, there are multiple elements that we need to explore and be conscious of in our planning and teaching. Ask teachers to examine the framework and identify what they are already using in the classroom and why these elements are necessary for supporting differentiation.

It is important for teachers to realize that this is not a linear model. Rather, all the elements are essential, and we need to work continually on some or all of them, keeping many balls in the air at once (Figure 19).

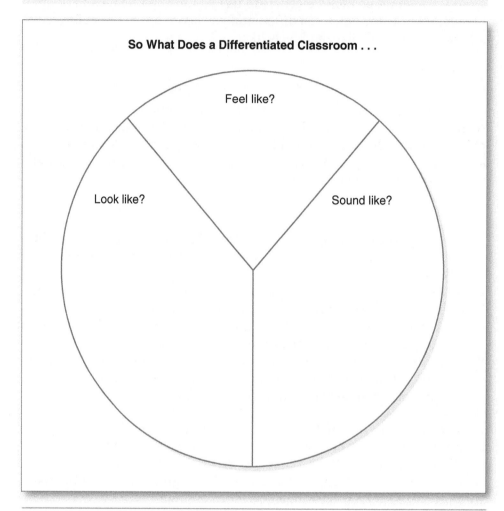

So What Does a Differentiated Classroom . . .

Feel like?

Look like?

Sound like?

Teachers may want to put green dots on familiar, already-used strategies or techniques and to highlight with yellow the ones that they would like to know more about. They may also want to identify one area that interests them, set a realistic goal for implementation, create some beginning steps, and set a timeline. A differentiation journal or a double-duty log (see Figure 11 in Chapter I-2) may be started at this time to facilitate reflection and to begin a chronicle of the journey into differentiation.

Using the Six-Step Planning Model for Differentiation

Present the Six-Step Planning Model (Figure 20). Discuss the designing-down process and the six steps in planning:

1. Set standards.

2. Define content.

Figure 18   Tools and strategies for designing inclusive differentiated classrooms for diverse learners

Climate	Knowing the Learner	Assessing the Learner	Adjustable Assignments	Instructional Strategies	Curriculum Approaches
Safe	**Learning Styles**	**Before**	**Compacting**	**Brain/Research Based**	**Centers**
Nurturing	Dunn & Dunn Gregorc	*Formal*	**TAPS**	Memory model	**Projects**
Encourages risk taking	Silver/Strong/Hanson	Pretest	*Total Group*	Elaborative rehearsal	**Problem-based learning**
	Multiple Intelligences	*Informal*	Lecturette	Focus activities	**Inquiry**
Multisensory	Using observation	Journaling	Presentation	Graphic organizers	**Contracts**
Stimulating	checklists, inventories,	Squaring off	Demonstration	Compare and contrast	
	logs, and journals to	Boxing	Jigsaw	Webbing	
Complex	become more aware of	Graffiti facts	Video	Metaphorical thinking	
Challenging	how students learn		Field trip	Cooperative group learning	
Collaborative		**During**	Guest speaker	Jigsaw	
Team and class building		*Formal*	Text	Questioning	
		Journaling/portfolios	*Alone*	Cubing	
Norms		Teacher-made tests	Interest	Role-play	
		Checklists/rubrics	Personalized		
		Informal	Multiple intelligences		
		Thumb it	*Paired*		
		Fist of five	Random		
		Face the fact	Interest		
			Task		
		After	*Small Groups*		
		Formal	Heterogeneous		
		Posttest	Homogeneous		
		Portfolio/conferences	Task oriented		
		Reflections	Constructed		
		Informal	Random		
		Talking topics	Interest		
		Conversation			
		Circles			
		Donut			

Figure 19   Differentiated instruction means keeping many balls in the air at once

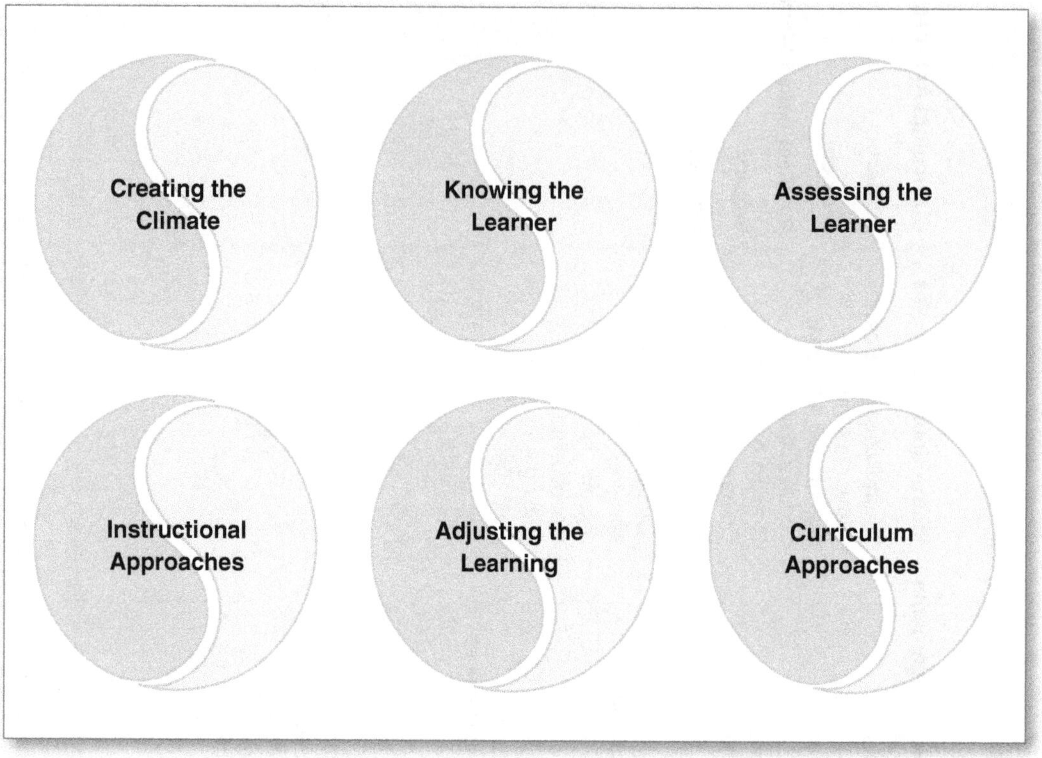

3. Activate prior knowledge.

4. Acquire new knowledge.

5. Apply and adjust the learning.

6. Assess the learning.

■ REFLECTIONS

1. In interest groups or alone, brainstorm ways you meet the individual needs of students. After compiling the list, post it and give it the title of "Ways to Differentiate Instruction."

2. Differentiated instruction is like _____ (select a noun) because _____ (list the many ways the two are alike). Illustrate, share, and post.

3. In groups of four, jigsaw the four ways to differentiate (1) content, (2) formative assessment, (3) performance assessment, (4) instructional strategies (pages 3–5). Each team member reads the section in the book on their assigned topic, takes notes, and adds how he or

Figure 20 The six-step planning model for differentiated learning template

Planning for Differentiated Learning	
1. **STANDARDS:** What should students know and be able to do?	Assessment tools for data collection (logs, checklists, journals, agendas, observations, portfolios, rubrics, contracts)
Essential Questions:	
2. **CONTENT:** concepts, vocabulary, facts	**SKILLS:**
3. **ACTIVATE:** Focus activity: Pre-assessment strategy Pre-assessment Prior knowledge and engaging the learners	• Quiz, test • Surveys • K-W-L • Journals • Arm gauge • Give me • Brainstorm • Concept formation • Thumb it
4. **ACQUIRE:** Total group or small groups	• Lecturette • Presentation • Demonstration • Jigsaw • Video • Field trip • Guest speaker • Text
5. **Grouping Decisions:** TAPS, random, heterogeneous, homogeneous, interest, task, constructed **APPLY** **ADJUST**	• Learning centers • Projects • Contracts • Compact/enrichment • Problem based • Inquiry • Research • Independent study
6. **ASSESS** Diversity honored (learning styles, multiple intelligences, personal interest, etc.)	• Quiz, test • Performance • Products • Presentation • Demonstration • Log, journal • Checklist • Portfolio • Rubric • Metacognition

she currently differentiates in that area. Then each participant shares his or her gathered information while the other group members take notes.

4. Use the chart on page 6. Take a personal inventory of current use of differentiated instruction. Place a star by the areas that you are implementing. Put a check by the areas that you have used, but not very often. Place an x by the areas that you have not used.

II-2

Creating a Climate for Learning

This chapter covers the fundamental elements that all learners need in order to succeed and to feel positive about their experiences in school. Strategies are based on *Differentiated Instructional Strategies: One Size Doesn't Fit All* (3rd ed.; Gregory & Chapman, 2013, pp. 13–22); page numbers enclosed in parentheses throughout this chapter refer to that book.

WHAT DO LEARNERS NEED TO SUCCEED? (PAGES 13–14) ■

Read pages 13–14, "What Do Learners Need to Succeed?" and "Teacher Mindsets." Examine the chart with Feedback for Success and Feedback to Encourage (Figure 2.1). Identify the differences in language and how they affect the recipient. Ask teachers to create additional comments for each column.

Concept Formation (Taba, 1962, 1999)

1. Ask teachers to use self-sticking notes and to brainstorm conditions conducive to learning, one idea per note.

2. Ask teachers to share their ideas in small groups and organize the suggestions written on their self-sticking notes according to like attributes.

3. When they have the notes organized by like attributes, ask the teachers to label each of the groupings.

Some teachers use the acronym GROUP to remember the steps:

Generate

Re-examine

Organize by similarities

Use a label to identify group

Process and discuss

Read pages 14–17, "Classroom Culture and Learning Communities," and list the brain issues that necessitate a positive classroom environment. Ask teachers to reflect on what is present in their classrooms and a concrete focus they can take to increase positive atmosphere.

Emotions and Learning (Pages 17–19)

1. Invite teachers to compare their ideas with Maslow's (1954, 1968), Glasser's (1990), and Kohn's (1993).

2. Ask teachers to think of something they remember from high school and share it with a colleague. Have them discuss the emotions evoked, which are usually very positive or negative in nature. Emotions have a major impact on facilitating or inhibiting learning.

3. Show the video clip on climate from *Differentiating Instruction to Meet the Needs of All Learners.* Use the elementary video (Gregory & Chapman, 2002a) at the 9-minute mark or the secondary video (Gregory & Chapman, 2002b) at the 8:30 mark. (These are available at www.PD360.com.)

4. After showing the video, ask teachers to generate strategies for setting a classroom tone of acceptance and support.

Emotional Intelligence (Pages 19–20)

1. In small groups, have teachers read and discuss the five domains of Daniel Goleman's (1995, 1998) emotional intelligence.

2. Set up a Round the Room Brainstorming activity (Figure 21), giving each group a chart with one of the five domains (Figure 22).

3. One group at each chart will brainstorm ways to foster this competency in classrooms and then, at a signal, move on to the next chart. There they will read what the previous group wrote and will add more suggestions. At the signal they will move again until every group has attended each chart.

This strategy is an excellent one for collegial problem solving and generating ideas, thus fostering the learning community. It can also be used with the framework for the six elements of differentiation (Figure 18 in Chapter II-1), with one group working on a chart for each element to generate what teachers are already doing in each area.

Figure 21   Round the room brainstorming

1. Divide into groups, one group for each chart.
2. Each group should stand in front of a chart.
3. Choose a writer for each group.
4. Quickly brainstorm responses to the topic on the chart.
5. After a minute or two, and at the signal, move one chart to your right.
6. Quickly brainstorm at the new chart (2 minutes).
7. At the signal, move to the right and repeat.
8. When you reach the last chart, go back to the original chart to analyze the data. Select and/or prioritize, cluster, or eliminate.

Figure 22   Five domains of emotional intelligence

Self-Awareness	Managing Emotions	Self-Motivation	Empathy	Social Skills

Self-Regulation (Pages 20–21)

Read pages 20–21 and discuss ways to foster skills of self-regulation and its value as a 21st-century skill.

Classroom Climate (Pages 22–25)

1. Have teachers read the information about classroom climate on pages 22–25.

2. After the reading, have teachers discuss how they create a positive physical and emotional climate.

3. Ask the teachers to experiment with different types of music to set a mood for the learning. An action research inquiry could be "How does music affect the learning and the learner?"

4. Using a video such as a segment from *Good Morning Miss Toliver* (FASE productions), invite teachers to identify the techniques that

Figure 23

Language used	Possibility thinking
Sense of fun and novelty	Use of music and risk-free atmosphere

Miss Toliver uses to create a positive climate for learning. The four squares in Figure 23 may help teachers hone in on key aspects.

5. On page 24 is a list of energizing cheers. Make up actions for each one. Notice the energy and laughter that are created as this is done. Try them out with your students and see what results you get. They celebrate small steps or major accomplishments. They also help students support one another and build a positive learning community.

6. Use the questions on page 26 for discussion or reflection. If teachers are keeping a differentiation journal, these might be prompts for consideration.

REFLECTIONS ◼

1. How would you describe your classroom climate?

2. How do you encourage team building throughout the year?

3. What do you do to create an atmosphere where students can take intellectual risks in your classroom?

4. How do you create intellectual safety and prohibit ridicule, put-downs, and other negative responses in your classroom?

5. How much wait time do you allow for thinking and answering questions?

6. What steps will you take to create an inclusive atmosphere where students feel safe and included?

7. How is "relaxed alertness" created?

8. How can you create "flow"?

II-3

Knowing the Learner

This chapter looks at how students differ in their learning styles and intelligences. Page references in parentheses are from *Differentiated Instructional Strategies: One Size Doesn't Fit All* (3rd ed.; Gregory & Chapman, 2013).

LEARNING PROFILES (PAGES 27–30) ■

A way of better knowing the learner is to create a learning profile that details the data about the student in a variety of areas and perspectives.

THE SWEET SPOT ■

Encourage participants to read pages 27–30 to better understand the notion/analogy of the Sweet Spot. Consider Figure 3.1 on page 28, and discuss how they as teachers are recognizing the following four areas:

Positive feelings

Prior successes

Interests

Attention

■ LEARNING PREFERENCES (PAGE 30)

1. After reading about the work of Dunn and Dunn (1987) on pages 30–31 and their three sensory learning preferences, invite teachers to work in small groups using a round robin technique. Teachers will pass around a graphic organizer (Figure 24) to brainstorm the types of instructional and classroom practices each learning style would appreciate.

2. As teachers pass the graphic organizer around the table, each person will act in turn as the recorder for one quadrant. This can also be done on butcher paper so that all can see and so that the groups may post their charts.

3. FLOW rules for brainstorming (Figure 25) may also be used for this process. This is a useful acronym for people to examine during brainstorming as it reminds them of the attributes of brainstorming and that speed and numerous ideas are important.

4. Teachers may also consider using the "How Do You Like to Learn?" survey (Figure 26). Ask them how they might use the survey or modify it for their students.

Figure 24   Graphic organizer for three learning styles round robin

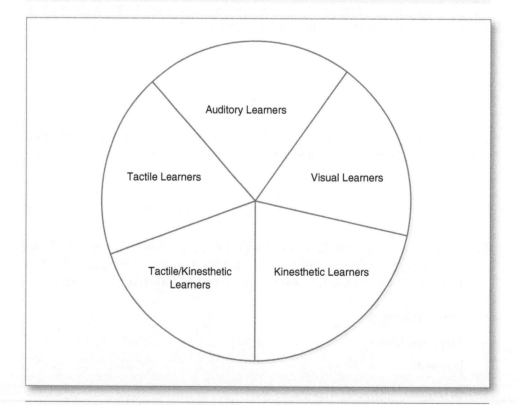

Figure 25   FLOW brainstorming

F	Free flow of ideas
L	Let all ideas come out, even "off the wall" ones
O	Originality counts
W	Weigh options later

SOURCE: Gregory (2005).

SO WHAT SHOULD WE DO ABOUT THAT? (PAGE 31)

This section suggests using multimodal forms of instruction rather than identifying and categorizing students.

Teachers should bring lesson plans and apply the questions on page 31 to ensure all modalities are included. Using Figure 3.3 on page 33, have teachers examine the ways information can be accessed and processed and how these provide a multimodal instructional program to meet the needs of all learners.

THINKING PREFERENCES (PAGES 35–39)

1. Ask teachers to read the section on thinking styles (pages 35–39) based on the work of Gregorc (1982), Kolb (1984), Sternberg (1996), and McCarthy (1990). Encourage a discussion about the similarities among the theories.

2. Ask teachers to consider the four commonly known items of beach ball, microscope, puppy, and clipboard, and decide which one they think is most representative of themselves.

3. After teachers share their decisions and reasons for choosing their items, invite them to go to one of the four corners of the room to match the item they selected (Figure 27). Each corner can be labeled with one of the four items: puppies, microscopes, clipboards, and beach balls.

4. Using a large sheet of paper, ask the teachers in each corner to brainstorm the attributes of this type of thinker and also the things that their type of learner would appreciate in the classroom. For example, puppies might say that they like people and would appreciate cooperative learning tasks.

5. Encourage the teachers to investigate learning styles further through reading additional resources and sharing their newfound information with others at another meeting.

Figure 26   How do you like to learn?

1. Do you like to have music on while you study, or do you prefer a quiet place?
    Quiet   Music

2. Where would you prefer to work on an assignment?
    Classroom   Desk (home)
    On the floor   At a table
    On a computer

3. If you are not able to complete something, is it because
    You forgot?   You are bored?
    You got distracted?   You need help?

4. Where do you like to sit in class?
    Near the door   Front
    By the wall   Near a window
    Back

5. How do you like to work?
    By yourself   With a partner
    In a small group

6. Are you more alert in the afternoon? In the evening? In the morning?

7. What classes do you enjoy most and why?

    _____

    _____

    _____

8. Describe how you study. Where? When? How?

    _____

    _____

    _____

9. If you have an assignment due in 2 weeks, how do you plan to complete it?

    _____

    _____

    _____

10. If something is new for you, do you
    Like to have it explained?   Like to read about it?
    Like to watch a video/demonstration?   Like to just try it?

Figure 27   Four corners activity for learning styles and thinking styles

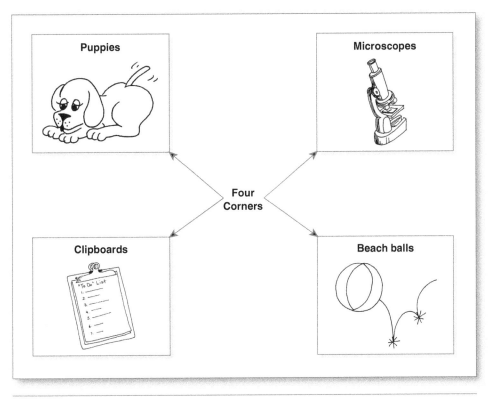

STERNBERG'S SUCCESSFUL INTELLIGENCE (PAGE 35–36) ■

As suggested in Sternberg's theory, consider Figure 3.5 and how it can be applied to products and projects related to core standards.

MULTIPLE INTELLIGENCES (PAGES 40–50) ■

1. After reading this section, ask teachers to speculate how they incorporate multiple intelligences in the classrooms.

2. Encourage teachers to begin with themselves and become more metacognitive about their own multiple intelligences. Using the "How Are You Intelligent?" chart (Figure 28), ask teachers to check off the statements that most represent them.

3. Photocopy the "What Is Your Unique Multiple Intelligences Profile?" chart (Figure 29) on a variety of colored sheets of 8.5x11-inch paper.

4. Ask the teachers to create their profiles by transferring the number of items that they checked in each category of Figure 28 to the

Figure 28   How are you intelligent?

Verbal/Linguistic Intelligence	**Intrapersonal Intelligence**
• I like to tell jokes, stories, or tales. • Books are important to me. • I like to read. • I often listen to radio, TV, tapes, or CDs. • I write easily and enjoy it. • I quote things I've read. • I like crosswords and word games.	• I know about my feelings, strengths, and weaknesses. • I like to learn more about myself. • I enjoy hobbies by myself. • I enjoy being alone sometimes. • I have confidence in myself. • I like to work alone. • I think about things and plan what to do next.
Logical/Mathematical Intelligence	**Visual/Spatial Intelligence**
• I solve math problems easily. • I enjoy math and using computers. • I like strategy games. • I wonder how things work. • I like using logic to solve problems. • I reason things out. • I like to use data in my work to measure, calculate, and analyze.	• I shut my eyes and see clear pictures. • I think in pictures. • I like color and interesting designs. • I can find my way around unfamiliar areas. • I draw and doodle. • I like books with pictures, maps, and charts. • I like videos, movies, and photographs.
Interpersonal Intelligence	**Bodily/Kinesthetic Intelligence**
• People ask me for advice. • I prefer team sports. • I have many close friends. • I like working in groups. • I'm comfortable in a crowd. • I have empathy for others. • I can figure out what people are feeling.	• I get uncomfortable when I sit too long. • I like to touch or be touched when talking. • I use my hands when speaking. • I like working with my hands on crafts/hobbies. • I touch things to learn more about them. • I think of myself as well coordinated. • I learn by doing rather than watching.
Musical/Rhythmic Intelligence	**Naturalist**
• I like to listen to musical selections. • I am sensitive to music and sounds. • I can remember tunes. • I listen to music when studying. • I enjoy singing. • I keep time to music. • I have a good sense of rhythm.	• I enjoy spending time in nature. • I like to classify things into categories. • I can hear animal and bird sounds clearly. • I see details when I look at plants, flowers, and trees. • I am happiest outdoors. • I like tending to plants and animals. • I know the names of trees, plants, birds, and animals.

relevant spot in Figure 29. After they finish, invite them to compare their profiles with each other to examine the differences in their strengths and areas of need.

5. Invite teachers to share how they get to know their students and also to examine Figures 30, 31, and 32 to see how they might use them for data collection and student awareness and reflection.

6. Another suggestion is to photocopy and laminate Figure 33 and use it when planning to spark ideas that may help teachers vary instruction and assessment and give students a choice in how they learn and show what they know.

7. Show the video *Differentiating Instruction to Meet the Needs of All Learners: Secondary Edition,* Tape 2, at the 34-minute point (Gregory & Chapman, 2002b). This section shows a secondary consumer science teacher who uses the inventory to help students assess their strengths and then offers them a choice in their assignment by selecting a project from a list of suggestions (see Gregory & Chapman, 2013, p. 168, for a sample list from the Nutrition and Wellness Project. Also available at www.PD360.com).

8. Invite teachers to examine the choices in Figure 34 and consider how they might offer students choices in the areas of multiple intelligences.

9. Teachers may also want to select a topic and standards that they plan to teach in the near future. Using the organizer in Figure 35, they can fill in the topic and learning goals targeted. Then, with a partner, they can brainstorm possibilities for learning and assessment in the eight intelligences that could be used in the classroom. After the brainstorming, teachers may examine and critically select those that they think would be most effective for the students with whom they are working.

10. Teachers also may want to consider setting up a contract system using some of these options (see Figures 36 and 37; see also pages 182–185).

GENDER DIFFERENCES (PAGES 50–51)

Read chart on page 51 outlining the differences in the brains of boys and girls. Examine the list on pages 50–51 with suggestions for honoring the brains of males and females. Make some plans to respond to those needs in your classroom.

CULTURAL DIFFERENCES (PAGE 52)

After reading and discussing the ways to be sensitive to cultures in the classroom, do an inventory of how you access and include different cultures.

Figure 29   What is your unique multiple intelligences profile?

Word Smart						
Math Smart						
People Smart						
Music Smart						
Self Smart						
Picture Smart						
Body Smart						
Nature Smart						

SOURCE: Adapted with permission from *Integrating Curricula With Multiple Intelligences: Teams, Themes, and Threads,* by Robin Fogarty and Judy Stoehr. © 1995 Corwin. www.corwin.com.

Figure 30 Teachers can capture observations over time about students'
multiple intelligences and transfer them to student profiles

Student Profile	
Observing over time . . .	Name:
Verbal/Linguistic	Intrapersonal
Logical/Mathematical	Visual/Spatial
Interpersonal	Bodily/Kinesthetic
Musical/Rhythmic	Naturalist

Figure 31   Eight intelligences: Self-reflection tool used by students individually or with peers

Complete this page and compare your answers with your partner.

If I could do anything I like, I'd . . .

Usually, when I have free time I . . .

My hobbies are . . .

At school I like to . . .

The type of things that we do in class I really like are . . .

I am uncomfortable when people ask me to . . .

Do you like to work alone or with a group? Why?

Figure 32   Yes—maybe—no list

1.

2.

3.

4.

5.

6.

7.

8.

9.

10.

Ask students about a variety of activities that they might have the opportunity to do.

How do you feel about . . .

1. Drawing and artwork?

2. Musical activities?

3. Working with others?

4. Working alone?

5. Using numbers?

6. Writing? Talking?

7. Dancing, sports, moving while learning?

8. Solving problems?

9. Reading?

10. Thinking about things?

11. Working with technology?

12. Being a leader?

Figure 33   Suggestions for using the eight multiple intelligences

Verbal/Linguistic

Brainstorming.
Organizing thoughts.
Summarize.
Change the beginning or the end.
Describe it.
Write an advertisement.
Write an editorial.
Write a news flash.
Prepare a speech.
Develop a campaign platform.
Develop a challenging question.
Find evidence to support a claim or
    belief.
This is like _____ because _____.
Research the inventor or an author.
Write a conclusion, summary.
Write main idea and supporting details.
Develop a book.
Record reading or writing.
Skim and scan.
Write the attributes.
Write adjectives or phrases
    to describe.

Musical/Rhythmic

Create a song.
Think of a theme song and say why.
Write a poem.
Create a jingle or slogan.
Select sounds to fit.
Recognize pitch, tone, timbre.
Use background music.
Create a beat.
Make rhythmic movements.
Identify sounds.
Identify musical pieces.
Interpret a song.
Record music.
Develop an instrument.
Find the background music

Logical/Mathematical

Sequence it.
Design a game.
Develop a TV show.
Create a timeline.
Tell your process.
Categorize.
Find the missing piece or link.
Classify.
Rank ideas.
Use a matrix.
Design a graph.
Try a new idea against a model.
Survey.
Conduct an inventory.
Research and gather data.
Interpret data.
Technology world.
Gadget use.
Compute or calculate.
Use deductive thinking.
Use numbers.

Visual/Spatial

Draw a picture or graphic.
Make a flip book.
Create a photo essay.
Design a poster.
Design a puppet.
Depict the setting.
Make a collage.
Illustrate it.
Plot on a graphic organizer.
Design or create.
Associations, recognitions, and use of
    color.
Use different art media.
Interpreting of art.
Design a book.
Sculpt it!
Make a flip book.
Draw a map and label sites of
    importance.
Develop a diorama.
Design a collage.
Highlight or tabbing.
Develop a character sketch.
Develop an editorial cartoon.
Write a cartoon strip with speech
    bubbles.
Color code.

Bodily/Kinesthetic

Movement.
Name its function.
Brainstorm.
Use your body to interpret meaning.
Play a game or sport.
Use manipulative.
Construct or build.
Role-play.
Perform.
Act it out.
Mime.
Puppet show.
Show how you know.
Dramatize.
Create simulations.
Interpretive dance.
Do an experiment.
Invent or discover through trial
    and error.

Interpersonal

Work with others.
Empathetic with others.
Work on a group project.
Conduct an interview.
Discuss with others.
Be involved in a conversation.
Come to a consensus.
Give or receive feedback.
Jigsaw information.
Be a team member.

Intrapersonal

Select personal choice.
Work alone.
Metacognitive thinking.
Plan a way.
Get a strategy.
Draw a conclusion about how it makes
    you feel.
Identify likes and dislikes.
Make choices.
Set goals.
Carry through a task.
How does it feel?
Identify your personal preference.
Automaticity.

Naturalist

Surviving.
Understanding nature.
Use nature to work for you.
The study of science.
Apply information to life.
Make a personal link and connection
    from your world.
Survival needs and awareness
    of them.
Identify scientific method and
    classifications.
Study of land, sea, and air.
Making discoveries.
Inventing.
Exploring the world.

Figure 34   Suggestions for Using the Eight Multiple Intelligences

Verbal/Linguistic
Prepare a report.
Write a play or essay.
Create a poem or recitation.
Listen to an audiotape on . . .
Interview.
Label a diagram.
Give directions for . . .

Bodily/Kinesthetic
Create a role-play.
Construct a model or representation.
Develop a mime.
Create a tableau for . . .
Manipulate materials.
Work through a simulation.
Create actions for . . .

Musical/Rhythmic
Compose a rap song or rhyme.
Create a jingle to teach others.
Listen to musical selections about . . .
Write a poem.
Select music or songs for a particular
purpose.

Interpersonal
Work with a partner or group.
Discuss and come to conclusions.
Solve a problem together.
Survey or interview others.
Dialogue about a topic.
Use cooperative groups.

Naturalist
Discover or experiment.
Categorize materials or ideas.
Look for ideas from nature.
Adapt materials to a new use.
Connect ideas to nature.
Examine materials to make
generalizations.

Logical/Mathematical
Create a pattern.
Describe a sequence or process.
Develop a rationale.
Analyze a situation.
Critically assess . . .
Classify, rank, or compare . . .
Interpret evidence . . .
Timeline.

Visual/Spatial
Draw a picture.
Create a mural or display.
Illustrate an event.
Make a diagram.
Create a cartoon.
Paint or design a poster.
Design a graphic.
Use color to . . .

Intrapersonal
Think about and plan.
Write in a journal.
Review or visualize a way to do
something.
Make a connection with past information
or experiences.
Metacognitive moment.

Figure 35   Brainstorming multiple intelligence choices

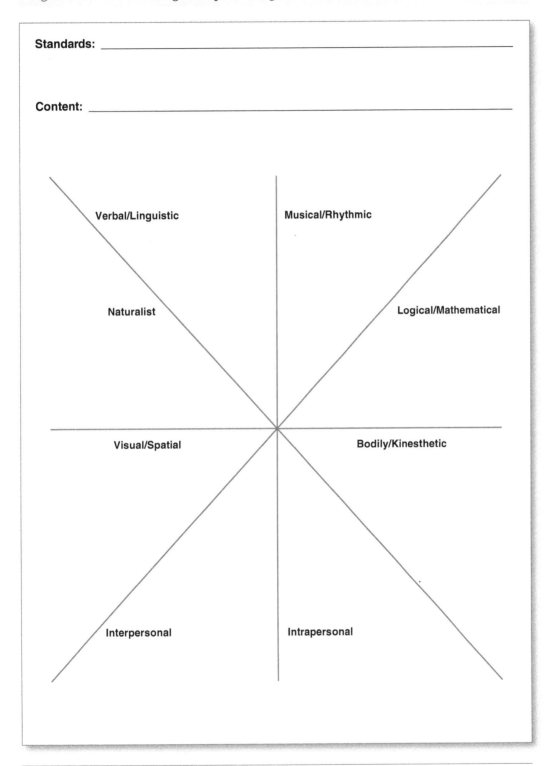

Standards: _____

Content: _____

Verbal/Linguistic

Musical/Rhythmic

Naturalist

Logical/Mathematical

Visual/Spatial

Bodily/Kinesthetic

Interpersonal

Intrapersonal

Figure 36   Contract form student fills in after choosing an activity

Name _____   Unit of Study _____

I agree to complete the following activity: _____

I chose this option because _____

_____

Please outline your plan: _____

_____

_____

_____

_____

_____

_____

_____

_____

_____

_____

By (date)

_____

Signature

_____

Figure 37   Contract form in which the teacher provides some core activities

Author Study Contract

To help improve your reading and writing, you will complete the core activities and may choose any optional activities that total at least 40 points.

Please fill in the contract and hand it in by _____.

Core Activities That Everyone Will Do: (Points)

1. I will select and begin a book by _____. (5)

2. I will create a "mind map" character sketch about a main character in my book (appearance, personality, friends/family, likes/dislikes). (10)

3. Each author uses language in interesting ways. Select three passages that you think are unique and explain in your own words their meaning and why you think the author expressed himself or herself in this way. (10)

Optional Selections:

4. I will write a one-page dialogue that I could role-play about a situation or problem that I read. (10)

5. I will draw a story map or comic strip with captions outlining the plot. (10)

6. I will write a commercial, design a poster, or produce a brochure on the computer to advertise my book and/or the author. (5)

7. As a critic, I will write an article sharing my thoughts about the story, outlining what I thought was Plus, Minus, and Interesting (de Bono, 1987). This will be a full-page column. I will use the word-processing program on the computer. (10)

8. I will design an option and discuss with the teacher. This will give me _____ points. (5 or 10)

Signed by Student

_____

Signed by Teacher

_____

■ POP CULTURE DIFFERENCES (PAGE 52)

Create a survey to get information about the pop cultures that are prevalent in your classroom.

■ REFLECTIONS

1. How do you get to know your students? What methods do you use?

2. How do you stimulate your students' strongest intelligences? How do you encourage students to cultivate their other intelligences?

3. How could you develop awareness about multiple intelligences with students and parents?

4. Use the suggestions in Figure 3.14 to check that learning styles and multiple intelligences are varied.

5. As you examine your lessons and units, are the needs of male and female students respected?

6. What cultures are represented, and what do you know about them?

7. Does your curriculum include opportunities to connect with all cultures present in your classroom and school?

8. What are the pop culture interests of your students? What bridges can you build?

II-4

Assessing the Learner

The Big Question that this chapter asks is "How does or should differentiated instruction impact assessment and evaluation?" Page references in parentheses are from *Differentiated Instructional Strategies: One Size Doesn't Fit All* (3rd ed.; Gregory & Chapman, 2013).

DEFINITIONS (PAGE 55) ■

1. To start, invite teachers to write in their own word definitions for the terms *assessment, evaluation,* and *grading* (Figure 38).

2. After teachers have written their own definitions, ask them to compare their definitions with those of Rolheiser, Bower, and Stevahn (2000) and with the discussion of assessment in *Differentiated Instructional Strategies: One Size Doesn't Fit All* (3rd ed.; Gregory & Chapman, 2013, pp. 55–56).

PURPOSES OF PRE-ASSESSMENT (PAGE 56) ■

1. As a group, ask teachers to list and discuss the merits of pre-assessing students (Figure 39).

2. Facilitate a dialogue focusing on all the positive reasons they've listed.

3. Move the discussion to the important follow-up question: With all those positive reasons for pre-assessing students, why isn't pre-assessment more widely practiced?

Figure 38   Defining assessment and evaluation

Assessment means . . .
Formative assessment means . . .
Portfolio is . . .
E-portfolio is . . .
Pre-assessment is . . .
Summative assessment is . . .
Evaluation means . . .
Grading means . . .

Figure 39   The merits of pre-assessment

Pre-assessment is important because . . .
–
–
–
–
–
–

PRE-ASSESSMENTS (PAGES 58–63) ◼

1. Show the pre-assessment section from one of the videos on *Differentiating Instruction to Meet the Needs of All Learners.* If you use the elementary edition (Gregory & Chapman, 2002a), show Tape 1, at the 21-minute mark (pre-assessment and assessment) and/or 4–11:30 minutes (pre-assessment). If you use the secondary edition (Gregory & Chapman, 2002b), show Tape 2 on pre-assessment using mind maps at the 4-minute mark. (Available at www.PD360.com.)

2. Ask teachers to list the pre-assessment techniques shown in the video they have just seen.

ASSESSMENT TOOLS TO USE BEFORE, DURING, AND AFTER LEARNING (PAGES 58–74) ◼

1. Ask teachers to select a partner for this activity, which will involve looking at several types of informal pre-assessment before, during, and after each lesson.

2. Assign the activities to the partners, choosing from the following selection:

   - Squaring Off
   - Boxing
   - Yes/No Cards
   - Graffiti Facts

SURVEYS (PAGES 63 AND 68) ◼

1. Review the sample interest survey questions on pages 54–56. You can call them a, b, and c and discuss the usefulness of surveys (Figures 40a, 40b, and 40c).

2. Ask the teachers to think about a survey that they might use for an upcoming unit of study. This survey may uncover interests as well as how students may want to learn the lesson content and with whom they may wish to work.

During the Learning (Pages 68–70)

- Thumb It
- Fist of Five
- Face the Fact
- Reaching for the Top
- Speedometer Reading

After the Learning (Pages 70–74)

- Wraparounds
- Talking Topics

- Conversation Circles
- Donut
- Rotation Reflection
- Paper Pass
- Grand Finale Comments

3. With their partners, teachers will demonstrate one of the informal assessments to the group and suggest when they might use it.

Figure 40a   Sample interest survey questions

	Rarely Ever	Sometimes	Most of the Time
1 I like to make up songs.	_____	_____	_____
2. I like to try things that are hard to do.	_____	_____	_____
3. Brain puzzles hold my interest.	_____	_____	_____
4. I like to take things apart and assemble them.	_____	_____	_____
5. I enjoy creating.	_____	_____	_____
6. I need manipulatives to learn.	_____	_____	_____
7. I am a follower.	_____	_____	_____
8. I am a leader.	_____	_____	_____
9. I prefer to work alone.	_____	_____	_____
10. I like to read.	_____	_____	_____
11. I prefer to work with others.	_____	_____	_____
12. I like to draw my own pictures.	_____	_____	_____
13. I can see visual images in my head.	_____	_____	_____
14. I have at least one pet.	_____	_____	_____
15. I enjoy animals.	_____	_____	_____
16. I would rather be outside than inside.	_____	_____	_____
17. I would rather be inside than outside.	_____	_____	_____
18. I like school.	_____	_____	_____
19. I do not like school.	_____	_____	_____
20. School would be better if . . .	_____	_____	_____
21. If I have free time, I prefer to	_____	_____	_____
a. _____	_____	_____	_____
b. _____	_____	_____	_____
c. _____	_____	_____	_____
22. I do not like _____ because _____.	_____	_____	_____
23. Additional comments	_____	_____	_____
a. _____	_____	_____	_____
b. _____	_____	_____	_____

Figure 40b   Math interest survey

Name: _____

Address: _____

Home Phone:_____

Date: _____

Course: _____

Please help me get to know you better.

1. My top two or three favorite activities are _____

2. Other activities that I like to do are _____

3. My favorite subject is _____

4. In my free time, I _____

5. On TV, I like to watch _____

6. The music I listen to is _____

7. I think a teacher should _____and _____

8. My favorite movies are _____and _____

9. I like my family because _____

10. I dislike school because _____

11. I like school because _____

12. Friends are important because _____

13. The most interesting person whom I have met is _____

    because _____

14. My chores at home are _____

15. My job outside of school is _____. How often? _____

16. I volunteer at _____. How often? _____

17. If I had $500, I would _____

18. I am in this math class because _____

19. I think this class will be (easy/difficult) because _____

20. I am excited about this class because _____

21. I am fearful of this class because _____

22. The things I will do in this class to be successful are _____

23. The things that may prevent me from being successful are _____

24. Something that I want you to know about me is _____

25. Any additional comments: _____

Figure 40c   Foreign language interest inventory (getting to know you)

Name: _____

Address: _____

Home Phone: _____

Date: _____

Course: _____

Please help me get to know you better.

1. My top two or three favorite activities are _____

2. Other activities that I like to do are _____

3. My favorite subject is _____

4. In my free time, I _____

5. On TV, I like to watch _____

6. The music I listen to is _____

7. I think a teacher should _____ and _____

8. My favorite movies are _____ and _____

9. I like my family because _____

10. I dislike school because _____

11. I like school because _____

12. Friends are important because _____

13. The most interesting person whom I have met is _____

14. My chores at home are _____

15. If I had $500, I would _____

16. I am in this Spanish class because _____

17. I think this class will be (easy/difficult) because _____

18. I am excited about this class because _____

19. I am fearful of this class because _____

20. The things I will do in this class to be successful are _____

21. The things that may prevent me from being successful are _____

22. Something that I want you to know about me is _____

23. Any additional comments: _____

ONGOING FORMATIVE AUTHENTIC ASSESSMENT TASKS (PAGES 74–76) ■

Review the list of authentic tasks in Figure 41. Organize a discussion around the following questions:

1. What is critical in planning so that these activities are not just fun and engaging but offer students experiences that provide real learning?

2. How could these activities be differentiated further based on students' readiness, interest, level of independence, or learning styles?

3. Thinking about giving students a choice, what might be done to offer choices with realistic expectations for different students?

PORTFOLIOS (PAGES 76–78) ■

1. Encourage teachers to discuss portfolios as a method of assessing student learning. What are the advantages? Issues? Concerns?

2. Encourage teachers who are already using student portfolios to serve as valuable resources that other staff members may access for information, processes, and reflection tools.

3. Suggest other resources that teachers can use for student portfolios. Consider using *The Portfolio Organizer* (Rolheiser et al., 2000) or *Portfolios Across the Curriculum and Beyond* (Cole, Ryan, Kick, & Mathies, 2000).

GRADING (PAGE 78) ■

Another issue that concerns teachers who are moving toward more differentiated classrooms is grading. Organize a discussion around the following questions:

1. What is grading?

2. What is the purpose of grading?

3. How is our school's or system's grading process helpful to learning?

4. What might change as we differentiate instruction and assessment?

Figure 41   Authentic assessment activities

Make a mural

Plan a trip

Conduct a panel

Create a magazine

Develop a display

Create a talk show

Choreograph a dance

Create costumes

Draw a comic strip

Teach a lesson

Create a flow chart

Design a video

Complete a portfolio

Write lyrics for a song

Design a survey and interview

Conduct a demonstration

Illustrate a story

Create a puppet play

Design a bulletin board

Create a timeline on the computer

Role-play the story

Write a persuasive article

Develop an innovation to . . .

SOURCE: Reprinted from *Differentiated Instructional Strategies: One Size Doesn't Fit All*, by Gayle H. Gregory and Carolyn Chapman, pp. 53–54. Thousand Oaks, CA: Corwin, © 2002. www.corwin .com.

REFLECTIONS ■

1. How do you currently pre-assess students?

2. How are you meeting the affective needs of your students? How do you incorporate the interests of your students into the learning experience? How do you combine these with prior knowledge and skills?

3. What data are you presently using to plan the instructional and assessment process?

4. What are you going to do first to improve assessment and feedback in your classroom?

5. Discuss feedback versus grading as a concept.

6. Are grading practices standardized and agreed upon in your school and/or grade level?

II-5

Adjusting, Compacting, and Grouping

Strategies are from *Differentiated Instructional Strategies: One Size Doesn't Fit All* (3rd ed.; Gregory and Chapman, 2013). Page numbers refer to that volume.

ADJUSTABLE ASSIGNMENTS (PAGES 83–89) ■

1. Ask teachers to define what we mean by *adjustable assignments*.

2. Challenge teachers to come up with an analogy for an adjustable assignment.

3. Use the Slinky analogy for an adjustable assignment (Figure 42). Ask teachers to list all the reasons that an adjustable assignment is like a Slinky.

4. Create a symbol that supports the Slinky analogy.

5. Screen the adjustable assignments section of the video *Differentiating Instruction to Meet the Needs of All Learners: Secondary Edition* (Gregory & Chapman, 2002b), Tape 2, at the 13-minute mark. (Available at www.PD360.com.)

6. Invite teachers to review the adjustable assignments section of the text on pages 83–89 and to then examine Figures 43 and 44.

Figure 42   Slinky analogy for adjustable assignments

An adjustable assignment is like a Slinky because

_____

_____

_____

_____

_____

_____

_____

_____. Create a symbol.

Pages 90–96 are samples of adjustable grids and lesson plans. Discuss the planning.

Adjusting Assignments

1. Ask teachers to form pairs or grade-level groups to create a chart on butcher paper as shown in Figure 45.

2. Suggest that teachers identify a standard or learning outcome and a topic or content to be studied.

3. Their next step is to identify a method of pre-assessing their students. Considering the standard or skill to be targeted:

   • What would be an appropriate pre-assessment technique?
   • Would an interest survey be applicable?
   • What formal or informal strategies could be used?

4. Teachers may then predict what learners may know or can do at perhaps three levels and log this information on Figure 45 in Section A.

5. Considering the data, what might be offered as a learning experience for students at the beginning level, the approaching level, and the high degree of competencies?

Figure 43   Sample adjustable assignment: Money

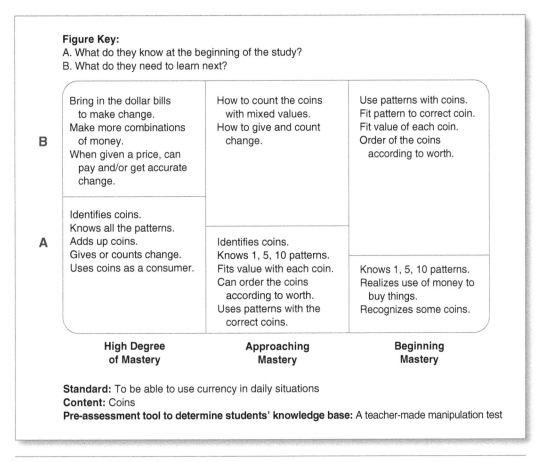

Figure Key:
A. What do they know at the beginning of the study?
B. What do they need to learn next?

B	Bring in the dollar bills to make change. Make more combinations of money. When given a price, can pay and/or get accurate change.	How to count the coins with mixed values. How to give and count change.	Use patterns with coins. Fit pattern to correct coin. Fit value of each coin. Order of the coins according to worth.
A	Identifies coins. Knows all the patterns. Adds up coins. Gives or counts change. Uses coins as a consumer.	Identifies coins. Knows 1, 5, 10 patterns. Fits value with each coin. Can order the coins according to worth. Uses patterns with the correct coins.	Knows 1, 5, 10 patterns. Realizes use of money to buy things. Recognizes some coins.
	High Degree of Mastery	**Approaching Mastery**	**Beginning Mastery**

Standard: To be able to use currency in daily situations
Content: Coins
Pre-assessment tool to determine students' knowledge base: A teacher-made manipulation test

6. Encourage teachers to follow the process in their classroom and experiment with the pre-assessment strategies and their instructional decisions based on the pre-assessment data.

Adjustable Review

1. At the next meeting, encourage teachers to share the outcomes of their experimentation through the examination of student work and reflection on their decisions.

2. Screen the video *Differentiating Instruction to Meet the Needs of All Learners: Elementary Edition* (Gregory & Chapman, 2002a), Tape 2, at the 132-minute mark, "Adjustable Review With Ellen Wilken," Grade 7 math teacher. (Available at www.PD360.com.)

3. Discuss how differentiating learning and respecting students are evident in this clip.

Figure 44   Sample adjustable assignment: Spanish

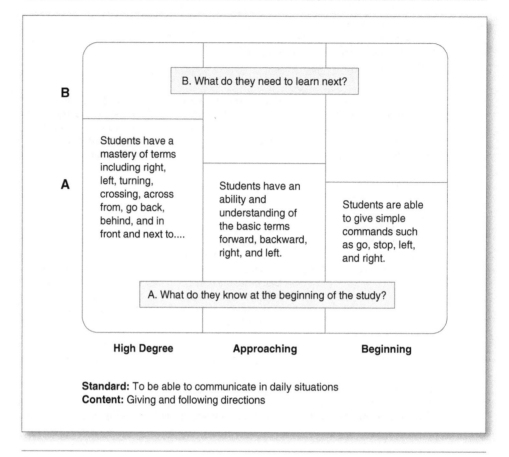

B. What do they need to learn next?

B

A

Students have a mastery of terms including right, left, turning, crossing, across from, go back, behind, and in front and next to....

Students have an ability and understanding of the basic terms forward, backward, right, and left.

Students are able to give simple commands such as go, stop, left, and right.

A. What do they know at the beginning of the study?

High Degree   **Approaching**   **Beginning**

Standard: To be able to communicate in daily situations
Content: Giving and following directions

■ RESPONSE TO INTERVENTION (PAGES 96–97)

As a group discussion, ask teachers to define the three tiers in the Response to Intervention model and where their team is in implementation of this direction. Have them make a plan for next steps.

■ CURRICULUM COMPACTING (PAGES 97–99)

1. Invite teachers to review the curriculum compacting section of the text on pages 97–99.

2. Facilitate a discussion focusing on the following questions:
   - What is compacting?
   - Why do we use it?
   - How do we do it?

3. Introduce the tactic Upside, Downside, On Side (Figure 46).

Figure 45   Adjustable assignment grid for recording data about student readiness levels

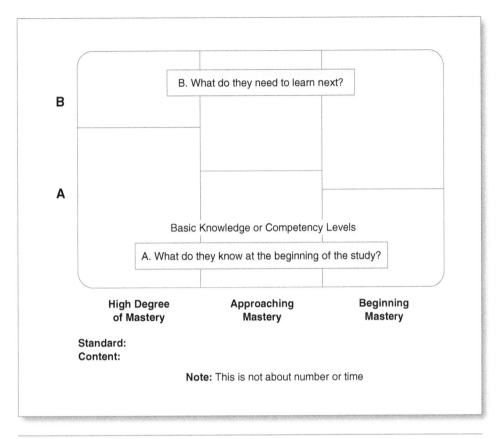

AGENDAS (PAGES 101–103)

Agendas help students and teachers use time well and keep track of accomplishments and progress. Ask teachers to examine the types shown on pages 101–102 and consider how they might use them. For an upcoming assignment or project, have them design an agenda that might work.

FLEXIBLE GROUPING (PAGES 103–111)

1. Ask teachers to take a few minutes to think about and discuss why and how students are grouped.

2. Consider TAPS (Figure 47) and the types of grouping that teachers use. Have them use Figure 48 to list when and how each type of group might be used.

Figure 46   Upside, downside, on side

Upside What are the positives for compacting?	
Downside What are the negatives associated with compacting?	
On side What have I already done related to compacting?	

Figure 47   TAPS

Total Group

  Alone

    Partner

      Small Group

TAPS (a rap)

Remember!

Some things need to be taught to the class as a whole.
There are certain things the Total Group should be told.

Working Alone, students get to problem-solve in their own way.
They will be in charge of what they think, do, and say.

With a Partner, many thoughts and ideas they can share.
They can work and show each other the solutions there.

Effective Small Groups work together to cooperate.
Using the group's ideas and talents, their learning will accelerate.

So use a variety of ways to group students you see.
This TAPS into students' potential, as it should be.

3. Invite teachers to work in pairs to create wallpaper posters (Figure 49) examining and clarifying one of the following small-group designs. These charts may be presented and discussed with colleagues.

   A. Knowledge of a subject (p. 105)
   B. Ability to perform a task or a skill (p. 106)
   C. Interests in a specific area of the content (p. 106)
   D. Peer-to-peer tutoring (p. 106)
   E. Cooperative learning (pp. 106–108)
   F. Sharing groups (pp. 108–111)

   - Energizing Partners
   - Brainstorming Bash
   - Total Class Brainstorming Bash
   - Adjustable Assignment Brainstorming Bash
   - Community Clusters
   - Content Talk

Figure 48   Using each type of group

Grouping Type	Used for
Total Group	
Alone	
Partner	
Small Groups	

Figure 49   Wallpaper poster clarifying small-group design

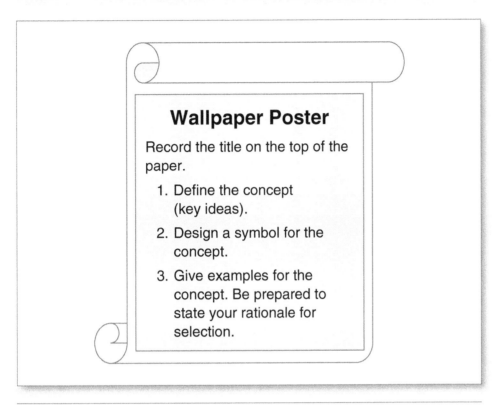

- Research Probes
- Experiment, Lab, Center, Station, or Project Groups

G.   Multiage grouping (p. 111)

Grouping Aids

1. Often "make and take" sessions may be held during lunchtime or in a short before-school meeting to actually construct things that would make life easier in the classroom.

2. Ask teachers to share ways of randomly grouping students. Provide time to construct "wagon wheel" teaming (Figure 50), based on the idea developed by Sheila Silversides (as cited in Kagan, 1992) for mixed-ability groups; learning styles (beach balls, clipboards, puppies, microscopes); or using student strengths in the multiple intelligences.

3. As an alternate or additional activity, teachers may use craft sticks or tongue depressors to create random groupings using the technique described in Figure 51.

Figure 50   Wagon wheel teaming: Rotating concentric circles to form teams of three or four learners at different levels

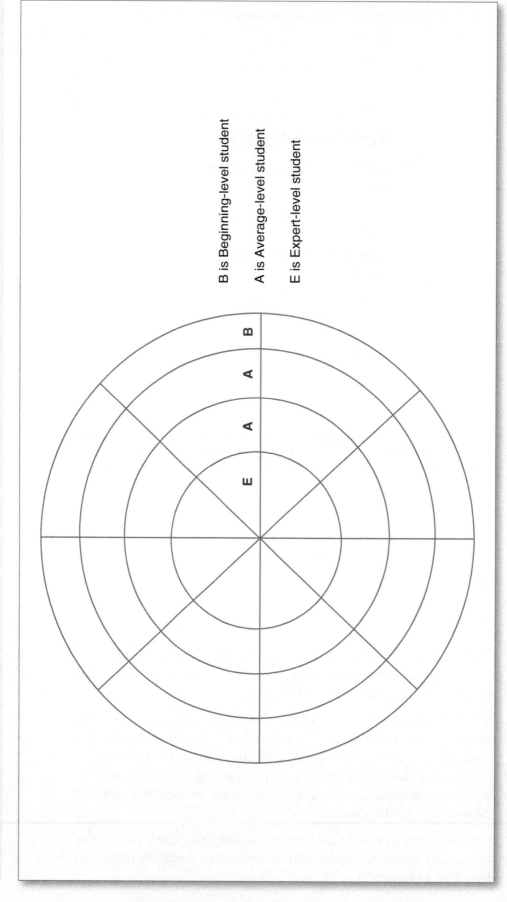

B is Beginning-level student

A is Average-level student

E is Expert-level student

Figure 51 Stick picks: Used to create random groups of heterogeneous learners

By using sticks you can efficiently and quickly create random groups. As students enter the class, hand each one a stick. The following list shows you the colors to put on each stick. Number the sticks and use magic marker to put the two colors on the stick. You can use craft sticks or tongue depressors. After you group the students, collect the sticks so that they are not lost or destroyed.

1	blue	orange
2	yellow	pink
3	red	purple
4	green	pink
5	yellow	orange
6	blue	purple
7	green	purple
8	red	pink
9	red	orange
10	green	orange
11	blue	pink
12	yellow	purple
13	yellow	purple
14	red	orange
15	green	pink
16	blue	pink
17	blue	purple
18	red	orange
19	yellow	orange
20	green	purple
21	red	pink
22	blue	purple
23	green	orange
24	yellow	pink
25	blue	pink
26	green	purple
27	red	orange
28	yellow	orange

(Continued)

Figure 51 (Continued)

29	yellow	pink
30	green	purple
31	blue	orange
32	red	pink
33	red	purple
34	yellow	purple
35	blue	pink
36	green	orange

Every group of four sticks (1–4, 5–8, etc.) has all four colors: green, yellow, blue, and red—one on each stick. If that group of four is a team, then the teacher can assign the roles based on the four colors green, yellow, blue, and red. Random groups can be formed by partnering students with the same two colors. Some groups will have two students, some three, and some four.

To get four larger groups, use the colors yellow, green, red, and blue as group identifiers.
To form three large groups, use the colors orange, pink, and purple.
To get partners, 1 and 2 are a pair, 3 and 4, 5 and 6, and so on.

■ REFLECTIONS

Consider a unit of work that you will be teaching in the near future.

1. What are the expectations or standards to be taught?

2. What assessment tools could you use to get data about students' prior knowledge, skills, and interests related to these standards?

3. Complete an adjustable grid to represent the information acquired that is related to the content or skill.

4. What instructional decisions will you make responding to the data that you have organized?

5. What group work is integrated into your students' day, week?

6. Is there a balance of TAPS configurations?

7. Are these structures consciously constructed or randomly evolved?

II-6

Instructional Strategies for Student Success

S trategies are from *Differentiated Instructional Strategies: One Size Doesn't Fit All* (3rd ed.; Gregory & Chapman, 2013). Page numbers refer to that volume.

RATIONALE FOR UNDERSTANDING HOW THE BRAIN WORKS (PAGE 114) ■

1. Present the following question for teachers to consider and discuss: If we can drive a car and not understand how engines operate and if we can use a DVD player and not know how to program it, why is it important to know about the brain?

2. In order to examine what we know about how the brain processes information, ask teachers to consider the following aspects of the process:

   - Attention
   - Memory
   - Context
   - Associating concepts
   - Rehearsal
   - Emotions
   - Recall and rehearsal

3. Using the same jigsaw strategy that also worked in Chapter I-2, refer to Figure 52. To facilitate the process, ask each person, pair, or small group to select one aspect of the process and to read, interpret, and teach the others about the concept by applying it to their experience in the classroom.

4. Use Figure 53 as an advance organizer, guide, and recording device.

5. Discuss the implications of this information for use in classrooms.

Focus and Sponge Activities (Pages 115–117)

1. Compare and contrast focus activities and sponge activities using a Venn diagram (Figure 54) or a Comparing Two Things flow chart (Figure 55).

2. Ask teachers to consider the suggestions on pages 115–117. Can they add to these based on their own experience?

Memory Processing Model (Page 120)

Using Figure 6.2 (page 120), partners will take turns explaining sensory memory, short-term working memory, and long-term memory.

Figure 52   Jigsaw strategies for advanced learners

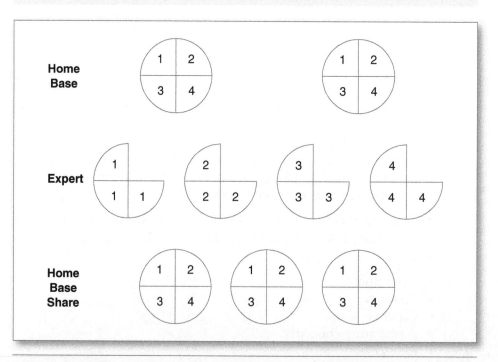

Figure 53   Advanced organizer for discussing how the brain works

Read, interpret, be ready to explain! Use examples where you can.	4. Attention (page 114)
1. Memory (page 117)	5. Rehearsal (page 118)
2. Context (page 118)	6. Emotions (page 118)
3. Associating concepts (page 119)	7. Recall and rehearsal (page 119)

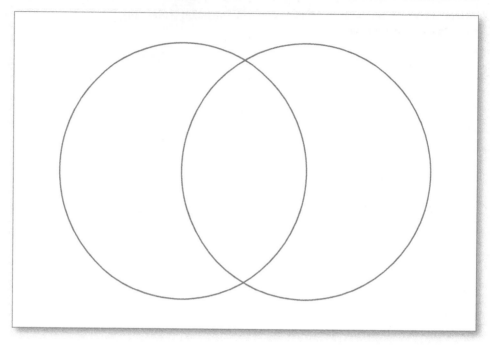

Figure 54   Venn diagram used to identify an area of overlap (similarities) between two topics

Planning Instructional Strategies (Page 121)

Review the questions related to the planning process on page 121.

Rehearsal Strategies (Pages 121–122)

To move information from short-term working memory to long-term memory, elaborative rehearsal is necessary. Multiple rehearsals are necessary to "hook" new information and skills in the neocortex and cerebellum. Examine the new research on evidence-based instructional strategies and the following three categories:

Creating the environment for learning: To engage the learner

1. Setting objectives and providing feedback

2. Reinforcing effort and providing recognition

3. Cooperative learning

Helping students develop understanding: For multiple rehearsals for understanding

4. Questions, cues, and advance organizers

5. Nonlinguistic representations

6. Summarizing and note-taking

7. Assigning homework and providing practice

Figure 55   Comparing two things flow chart

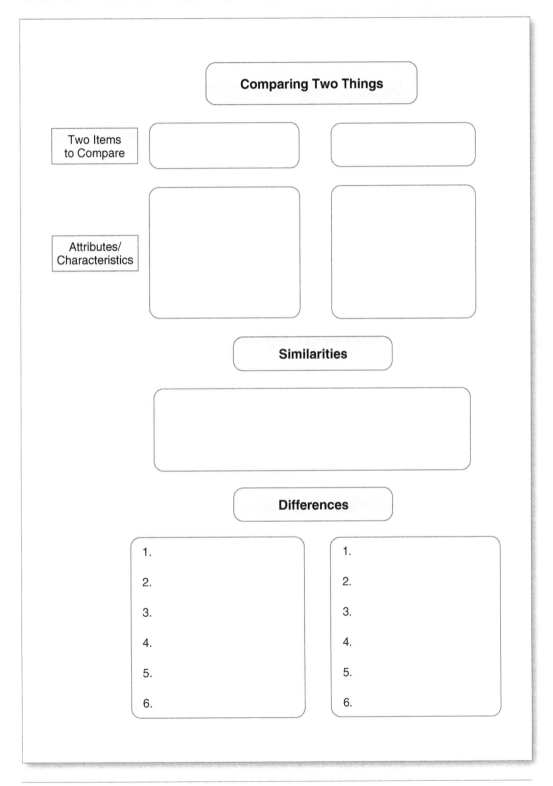

Helping students extend and apply knowledge: To extend thinking and possibilities

8. Identifying similarities and differences

9. Generating and testing hypotheses

Examine Figure 6.3 on page 123, and discuss how the eduneuroscience information supports the strategies that make a difference for student learning.

■ COOPERATIVE GROUP LEARNING (PAGES 122–131)

1. Have teachers explore the Web site of the Partnership for 21st Century Skills (www.p21.org) and identify these century skills. One of the essential skills is the ability to get along with others and work as a team. Cooperative group learning is a strategy that helps develop effective social skills, increase understanding and retention, and facilitate higher order thinking.

2. Ask teachers to discuss problems of students working collaboratively. As issues surface, time may be given for suggesting solutions to group work problems.

3. Review the TASK acronym (Gregory & Chapman, 2013; Robbins, Gregory, & Herndon, 2000) and facilitate a discussion focusing on those four aspects of cooperative group learning:

   Thinking is built into the process

   Accountability is essential; goal achievement: both individual and group

   Social skills for team success

   Keeping everyone on TASK: roles, tasks, resources, novelty, simulations, and clear expectations

4. How do we ensure that the four TASK aspects are implemented when we use cooperative group learning as a strategy?

5. Suggest that teachers use Figure 56 to create charts and brainstorm ways to ensure that we attend to the essential elements. Post the charts and invite teachers to do a wall walk so that they can see what others have suggested.

6. Reflect on the steps and questions for using cooperative group learning on pages 128–129.

■ JIGSAW (PAGES 129–131)

1. Facilitate a discussion about the jigsaw strategy and its uses.

2. Examine Figure 57 and suggest several variations that teachers might use for a character sketch. Or use Figure 58 on body systems, which may be used in a science or health class.

Figure 56 Implementing the TASK elements of cooperative group learning

Thinking Skills Are Built Into the Process
Accountability Is Essential
Social Skills for Team Success
Keeping Students on Task

3. Invite teachers to work in groups of four to complete Figure 59 about differentiated instruction, focusing on evidence of creating the climate, knowing the learner, assessing the learner, and adjusting assignments.

4. Challenge teachers to adopt or adapt this model for use with some topic or content in the next few weeks. Ask teachers to bring to the next meeting their sample plus examples of student work.

Figure 57   Character sketch: Used as an organizer by four students when reading a story or novel

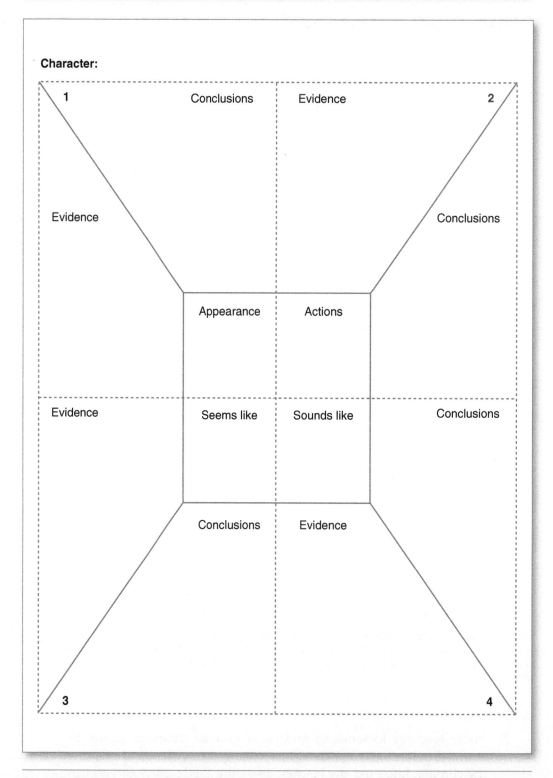

Figure 58   Body systems: Used as a graphic organizer in a science or health class

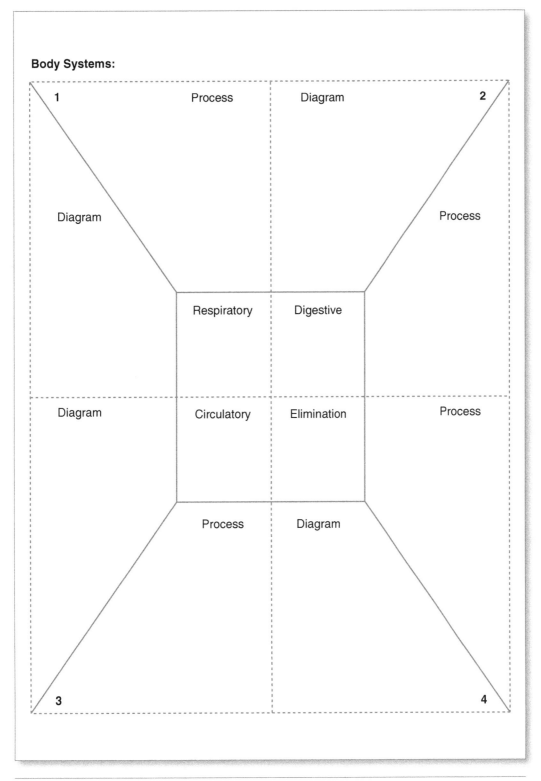

Figure 59   Graphic organizer for differentiated instruction

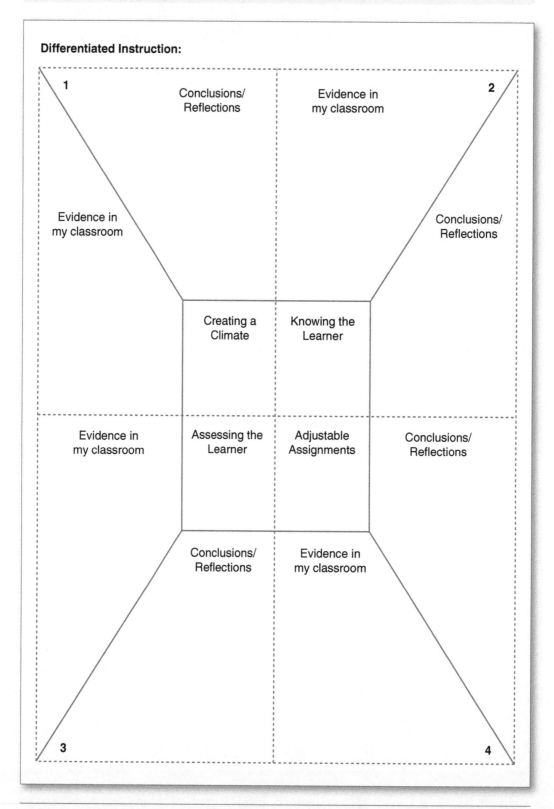

Differentiated Instruction:

1

Conclusions/
Reflections

Evidence in
my classroom

2

Evidence in
my classroom

Conclusions/
Reflections

Creating a
Climate

Knowing the
Learner

Evidence in
my classroom

Assessing the
Learner

Adjustable
Assignments

Conclusions/
Reflections

Conclusions/
Reflections

Evidence in
my classroom

3

4

Nonlinguistic Representations: Graphic Organizers (Page 131)

1. Ask teachers to reflect on their use of graphic organizers.

    *   How are they brain compatible?
    *   Which ones do teachers already use in the classroom?
    *   How do graphic organizers support multiple intelligence theory?

2. Have each teacher use a Venn diagram to suggest how they could have students compare two things to increase higher order thinking (Figure 54).

3. Using Figure 6.10 on page 135, ask teacher to create categories and criteria for a cross-classification chart that might be used by students in any subject discipline.

4. Ask teachers (alone or working in pairs) to select a graphic organizer from Figure 60.

5. After the selection, ask the teachers to use the organizer they have chosen in relation to the concept of differentiation to further develop their understanding and continued dialogue. Examples:

    *   *Fact Frame:* Write "Differentiation is important for students" in the center box. Write supporting details in the outer box.
    *   *Roll It:* Write "differentiation" in the tire section. Write four key points on the spokes.
    *   *Inside Out:* Write "differentiation" in the center. Write its attributes in the outer oval.
    *   *Angle Antics:* Put "differentiation" in the big triangle. Write the effects on each side of the triangle. Put "traditional" in the bottom triangle and the effects on each side.
    *   *Star Connections:* Put "differentiation" in the center and one positive outcome on the points of the star.
    *   *Drumming Up Details:* Write a prediction about differentiation on the top of the drum. State the outcomes or learned facts on the side of the drum.
    *   *Facts and Opinions:* Write a fact about differentiation in the center. List an opinion by each arrow.
    *   *3 and 3:* Write an important topic (differentiation and traditional) in each of the large triangles. Write the meaning, write a sentence, and draw a picture on the sidelines.
    *   *Summing It Up:* In the top rectangle, write a fact about differentiation. In the next two boxes, write two supporting details. Then write a summary or conclusion in the bottom figure.

METAPHORS (PAGE 109)

1. Ask teachers to think about the use of metaphors as an instructional strategy. Using metaphors is another way of using the thinking skill of compare-and-contrast.

Figure 60   Graphic organizer framework

Fact Frame	Roll It!	Inside Out!
Angle Antics	Star Connections	Drumming Up Details
Facts and Opinions	3 and 3	Summing It Up!

2. Review Figure 27 (Chapter II-3) about learning styles and thinking styles and Figure 42 (Chapter II-5) relating adjustable assignments to a Slinky. The power of an analogy or metaphor is that the concept is understood and its attributes are remembered better when it is related to a well-known object or idea. An analogy is a single concept that encompasses a large mental file of information.

3. Discuss how metaphors and analogies can be used in the classroom to increase understanding, memory retention, and higher order thinking using compare-and-contrast.

■ ROLE-PLAYING (PAGES 139)

1. Review the *why* and *how* of using this strategy.

2. Facilitate a discussion focusing on the following questions:

    • How is it brain compatible?
    • How might it be used in the classroom in a variety of subject areas to increase retention and understanding?

3. Screen the video *Differentiating Instruction to Meet the Needs of All Learners: Secondary Edition* (Gregory & Chapman, 2002b), Tape 2, at the 6–11:30 mark.

4. Ask teachers to list all of the instructional strategies that teachers in the video have used.

Instructional Technique: Questioning (Pages 140–145)

1. After reading the information about questioning, have teachers discuss their experience with questioning and the strategies they already use to differentiate questioning.

2. Teachers who are interested in beginning to differentiate questioning may want to use the question starters in Figure 61. Based on the different levels of Bloom's (1956) thinking taxonomy, these two columns of question starters and potential activities may be printed on a colored piece of paper with the paper folded lengthwise and laminated. Teachers can then hold this as a prompt during total class discussions to give them language to use in differentiating questions to individuals in the class.

3. After using the question starters for some time in classes, teachers may want to discuss their successes or problems with questioning at a later meeting.

Instructional Technique: Cubing (Pages 142–148)

1. Have teachers read the information about cubing on pages 142–148 for another strategy that provides a variety of ways to examine an idea or concept. After the reading, have teachers discuss how cubing can be used in their classrooms.

2. Show the video *Differentiating Instruction: Tape 2* (Tomlinson, 1998b), focusing on the end of the tape, which covers interest surveys, flexible grouping, and cubing. Give teachers an advance organizer (Figure 62) for collecting data and analyzing their reactions to the classroom scenario. (Also available at www.PD360.com.)

3. After viewing the video, encourage teachers to share data recorded on their advance organizers and discuss the uses of cubing in their classrooms.

4. Using large store-bought dice, have teachers take turns in small groups rolling the dice and responding to the concept of differentiation in relationship to the number that they roll (Figure 63).

How Can We Use Cubes?

1. In a planning meeting, ask teachers to review the five steps for using cubes on page 146:

   - Keep clear learning goals in mind.
   - Provide extended opportunities and materials appropriate for a wide range of readiness, interests, and learning styles.

Figure 61   Question starters and classroom activities differentiated according to Bloom's Taxonomy

QUESTION STARTERS

Level I: REMEMBER (recall)

1. What is the definition for . . . ?
2. What happened after . . . ?
3. Recall the facts.
4. What were the characteristics of . . . ?
5. Which is true or false?
6. How many . . . ?
7. Who was the . . . ?
8. Tell in your own words.

Level II: UNDERSTAND

1. Why are these ideas similar?
2. In your own words retell the story of . . .
3. What do you think could happen?
4. How are these ideas different?
5. Explain what happened after.
6. What are some examples?
7. Can you provide a definition of . . . ?
8. Who was the key character?

Level III: APPLICATION (applying without understanding is not effective)

1. What is another instance of . . . ?
2. Demonstrate the way to . . .
3. Which one is most like . . . ?
4. What questions would you ask?
5. Which factors would you change?
6. Could this have happened in . . . ? Why or why not?
7. How would you organize these ideas?

POTENTIAL ACTIVITIES

1. Describe the . . .
2. Make a time line of events.
3. Make a facts chart.
4. Write a list of . . . steps in . . . facts about . . .
5. List all the people in the story.
6. Make a chart showing . . .
7. Make an acrostic.
8. Recite a poem.

1. Cut out or draw pictures to show an event.
2. Illustrate what you think the main idea was.
3. Make a cartoon strip showing the sequence of . . .
4. Write and perform a play based on the . . .
5. Compare this _____with_____
6. Construct a model of . . .
7. Write a news report.
8. Prepare a flow chart to show the sequence . . .

1. Construct a model to demonstrate using it.
2. Make a display to illustrate one event.
3. Make a collection about . . .
4. Design a relief map to include relevant information about an event.
5. Scan a collection of photographs to illustrate a particular aspect of the study.
6. Create a mural to depict . . .

QUESTION STARTERS	POTENTIAL ACTIVITIES

Level IV: ANALYSIS

1. What are the component parts of . . . ?
2. What steps are important in the process of . . . ?
3. If . . . then . . .
4. What other conclusions can you reach about . . . that have not been mentioned?
5. The difference between the fact and the hypothesis is . . .
6. The solution would be to . . .
7. What is the relationship between . . . and . . . ?

1. Design a questionnaire about . . .
2. Conduct an investigation to produce . . .
3. Make a flow chart to show . . .
4. Construct a graph to show . . .
5. Put on a play about . . .
6. Review . . . in terms of identified criteria.
7. Prepare a report about the area of study.

Level V: EVALUATE

1. In your opinion . . .
2. Appraise the chances for . . .
3. Grade or rank the . . .
4. What do you think should be the outcome?
5. What solution do you favor and why?
6. Which systems are best? Worst?
7. Rate the relative value of these ideas to . . .
8. Which is the better bargain?

1. Prepare a list of criteria you would use to judge a . . . Indicate priority ratings you would give.
2. Conduct a debate about an issue.
3. Prepare an annotated bibliography . . .
4. Form a discussion panel on the topic of . . .
5. Prepare a case to present your opinions about . . .
6. List some common assumptions about . . . Rationalize your reactions.

Level VI: CREATE

1. Can you design a . . . ?
2. Why not compose a song about . . . ?
3. Why don't you devise your own way to . . . ?
4. Can you create new and unusual uses for . . . ?
5. Can you develop a proposal for . . . ?
6. How would you deal with . . . ?
7. Invent a scheme that would . . .

1. Create a model that shows your new ideas.
2. Devise an original plan or experiment for . . .
3. Finish the incomplete . . .
4. Make a hypothesis about . . .
5. Change . . . so that it will . . .
6. Propose a method to . . .
7. Prescribe a way to . . .
8. Give the book a new title.

Figure 62   Advance organizer for cubing lesson video

How did the teacher use interest surveys? What value did she see in them? What are your thoughts about interest surveys?	
How was flexible grouping used?	
What was differentiated in this lesson?	
What thinking skills were targeted? How were visual representations incorporated?	
What are your thoughts and ideas about the use of cubing?	

Figure 63   Rolling the dice

1. They describe it.

2. They compare it to a traditional instruction.

3. They associate it with other concepts.

4. They analyze the elements.

5. They apply it to their students.

6. They argue for or against it.

- Make sure students understand the verbs and task directions.
- Group students according to readiness, understanding, and ability levels.
- Ask students to share findings with the larger group or to form expert groups.

2. Teachers can work in pairs or small groups using Figure 64 (levels of thinking) and Figure 65 (interests) to develop a lesson or centers

Figure 64   Different verbs, tasks, and commands on each side of a cube show different levels of thinking

Cubing . . . Levels of Thinking	
1. Tell Describe Recall Name Locate List	4. Review Discuss Prepare Diagram Cartoon
2. Compare Contrast Example Explain Define Write	5. Propose Suggest Finish Prescribe Devise
3. Connect Make Design Produce Develop	6. Debate Formulate Choose Support In your opinion . . .

using cubing to differentiate instruction to meet the needs of students in their classrooms. They may also consider multiple intelligences (Gardner, 1983, 1993) in lesson planning.

USING TECHNOLOGY IN THE DIFFERENTIATED CLASSROOM (PAGES 149–150) ■

Read pages 149–150 and discuss the following:

- Need for professional development for technology
- Challenges and issues related to technology
- Technology you already use
- Technology you would like to incorporate
- How students can be encouraged to take the lead
- Use of e-folios, etc.
- Exploration of blogs, wikis, glossaries, feeds, polls, surveys, and assignments

Figure 65   Cubes vary in color and tasks depending on the prior knowledge and interest of the learners

Green Cube	Blue Cube
1.	1.
2.	2.
3.	3.
4.	4.
5.	5.
6.	6.
Yellow Cube	**Red Cube**
1.	1.
2.	2.
3.	3.
4.	4.
5.	5.
6.	6.

REFLECTIONS ■

1. Considering the Best Practice, Brain Research chart in Figure 6.3 (page 123), which strategies are you using on a routine basis?

2. Which instructional strategy will you incorporate into your repertoire in the next month?

3. How will you do that? With what content might you try it?

4. With whom could you work and plan for this implementation?

5. How will you monitor student improvement or reaction to the use of this strategy?

6. Brainstorm lists of focus activities and graphic organizers.

7. Design cubes for upcoming topics.

II-7

Curriculum Approaches for Differentiated Classrooms

S trategies are from *Differentiated Instructional Strategies: One Size Doesn't Fit All* (3rd ed.; Gregory & Chapman, 2013). Page numbers refer to that volume.

CENTERS (PAGES 153–163) ■

1. Considering centers as a curriculum model, what concerns surface when teachers think about utilizing centers in the classroom? These concerns usually focus on matters relating to design, management, and assessment.

2. Discuss these concerns, acknowledging that teachers who have experience with centers may be excellent resources for the larger group. It is often a great opportunity for middle and secondary teachers to be able to tap into their colleagues who teach in elementary schools, where centers are often more prevalent.

3. Discuss *design* concerns: Remind teachers that they need to consider standards and content objectives before designing the centers so that the centers are real learning experiences and not just "fun" experiences.

4. Discuss *management* concerns: Teachers may also consider and discuss the management procedures and techniques suggested on

page 157 and also share the techniques they have discovered that work well with students.

5. Discuss *assessment:* There are a variety of assessment tools on pages 159–160, including anecdotal findings, checklists, questioning techniques, and student self-assessments with metacognitive tools.

6. Use Figure 66 as a planning template. Ask teachers to work collaboratively to design centers that will reflect standards and increase students' knowledge and skills.

7. Teachers may also use Figure 67 as a resource for multiple intelligences ideas and activities to incorporate in their planning.

■ PROJECTS FOR DIFFERENTIATED CLASSROOMS (PAGES 163–171)

1. Invite teachers to use the triple Venn diagram in Figure 68 to compare and contrast projects that are structured, topic-related, and open-ended.

2. Encourage teachers to examine the project samples on pages 168–171 and to think about how this model may be adapted for use in their classrooms.

3. Review assessment strategies, including rubrics, on page 167.

4. Suggest that teachers also explore the RubiStar Web site (http://rubistar.4teachers.org), which will help them custom design rubrics for their projects.

Choice Boards (Pages 171–178)

Examine the different types of choice boards. Have teachers select a type that they think would be useful for a unit of study. They should identify a standard, topic, or content and create a choice board that will give students opportunities for choices and preferences and allow them to be creative and rehearse content and skills in a variety of ways.

Using Figure 69 for suggestions, ask teachers to design a multiple intelligences choice board by selecting one activity from each box and creating a choice board for a particular topic. Use an 8½x11-inch sheet folded in nine boxes.

■ PROBLEM-BASED LEARNING (PAGES 171–179)

1. Ask teachers to read pages 171–179 about problem-based learning.

2. Facilitate a discussion about problem-based learning, including these questions:

   • What is it?
   • Why do it?

Figure 66   Center planning template

Center: _____

Standards: _____

Content: _____

_____

_____

Who: _____

Activities

Assessment

Figure 67   Multiple intelligences: Suggestions for centers and projects

Verbal/Linguistic
Prepare a report.
Write a play or essay.
Create a poem or recitation.
Listen to an audiotape on . . .
Interview.
Label a diagram.
Give directions for . . .

Bodily/Kinesthetic
Create a role play.
Construct a model or representation.
Develop a mime.
Create a tableau for . . .
Manipulate materials.
Work through a simulation.
Create actions for . . .

Musical/Rhythmic
Compose a rap song or rhyme.
Create a jingle to teach others.
Listen to musical selections about . . .
Write a poem.
Select music or songs for a particular
purpose.

Interpersonal
Work with a partner or group.
Discuss and come to conclusions.
Solve a problem together.
Survey or interview others.
Dialogue about a topic.
Use cooperative groups.

Naturalist
Discover or experiment.
Categorize materials or ideas.
Look for ideas from nature.
Adapt materials to a new use.
Connect ideas to nature.
Examine materials to make
generalizations.

Logical/Mathematical
Create a pattern.
Describe a sequence or process.
Develop a rationale.
Analyze a situation.
Critically assess . . .
Classify, rank, or compare . . .
Interpret evidence . . .
Timeline.

Visual/Spatial
Draw a picture.
Create a mural or display.
Illustrate an event.
Make a diagram.
Create a cartoon.
Paint or design a poster.
Design a graphic.
Use color to . . .

Intrapersonal
Think about and plan.
Write in a journal.
Review or visualize a way to do
    something.
Make a connection with past
    information or experiences.
Metacognitive moment.

Figure 68   Triple Venn diagram to compare and contrast projects

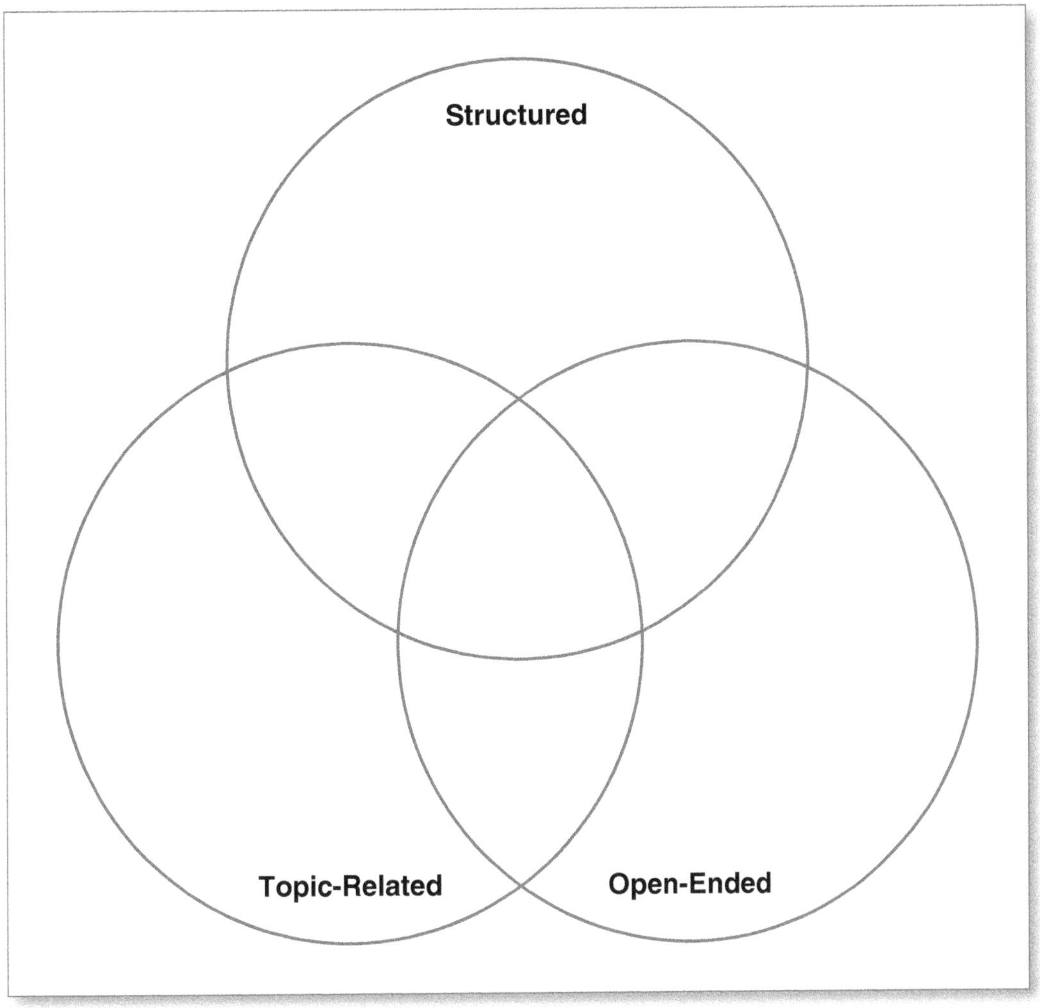

- How do you do it?
- What is it about problem-based learning that is brain compatible?
- How can problems be adjusted to suit different learners based on readiness, interest, or complexity?

3. Screen the video *Differentiating Instruction to Meet the Needs of All Learners: Secondary Edition* (Gregory & Chapman, 2002b), Tape 2, for the section showing a secondary teacher who is using problem-based learning with students in a science class. (Available at www .PD360.com.)

Figure 69   Multiple intelligences choice board

Verbal/Linguistic	Musical/Rhythmic	Visual/Spatial
Prepare a report Write a play or essay Give directions for . . . Create a poem or recitation Listen to a tape or view a video Retell in your own words Create a word web	Create a rap, song, or ballad Write a jingle Write a poem Select music to enhance a story or event Create rhymes that . . .	Create a mural, poster, or drawing Illustrate an event Draw a diagram Design a graphic organizer Use color to . . . Create a comic strip to show . . . Construct a storyboard Create a collage with meaningful artifacts
Logical/Mathematical Create a pattern Describe a sequence or process Develop a rationale Analyze a situation Create a sequel Critically assess Classify, rank, or compare Interpret evidence Design a game to show . . .	**Free Choice**	**Bodily/Kinesthetic** Create a role-play Construct a model or representation Develop a mime Create a tableau for . . . Manipulate materials to work through a simulation Create actions for . . .
Naturalist Discover or experiment Categorize materials or ideas Look for ideas from nature Adapt materials to a new use Connect ideas to nature Examine materials to make generalizations Label and classify Draw conclusions based on information Predict	**Interpersonal** Work with a partner or group Discuss and come to a conclusion Solve a problem together Survey or interview others Dialogue about a topic Use cooperative groups to do a group project Project a character's point of view	**Intrapersonal** Think about and plan Write in a journal Keep track of and comment on . . . Review or visualize a way Reflect on the character and express his or her feelings Imagine how it would feel if you . . .

4. Consider KWL and KND plans (pages 117 and 175).

   - What do you *know* about this problem?
   - What do you *need* to solve this problem?
   - What will you *do* to get what you need?

5. How might KND be a useful technique to use when students are working on a problem?

CONTRACTS (PAGES 180–187)

1. Using 3-2-1 (Figure 70) as a guideline, discuss contracts and their use in a differentiated classroom.

2. Screen the video *Differentiating Instruction to Meet the Needs of All Learners: Secondary Edition* (Gregory & Chapman, 2002b), Tape 2, 11:30-minute mark, showing a secondary teacher who is using Eight Choices for *Animal Farm*. (Available at www.PD360.com.)

3. Examine Figure 71 for examples of how teachers can use Eight Choices to plan a unit of study about World War II.

4. Discuss how teachers can use a generic planning template (Figure 72) to design a set of choices for a topic they might want to use with their students.

5. Encourage teachers to modify or adjust tasks in the framework to suit outcomes, student interests, multiple intelligences, and available resources.

CREATING OPPORTUNITIES TO DISCUSS DIFFERENTIATED INSTRUCTION

1. Use People Search (Bellanca & Fogarty, 1991; Gregory & Parry, 2006) at any time for a faculty meeting or study group activity to create opportunities to discuss aspects of differentiation.

2. Give each teacher a copy of the differentiation review in Figure 73. Encourage them to walk around the room sharing answers for the statements in each box. They are sure to listen attentively to each speaker.

3. Remind teachers to write down the name of each person who gives them information. Those colleagues can become valuable resources for discussion and reflection as the entire professional learning community moves toward differentiated instruction for all their students.

Figure 70   3-2-1 guide for planning contracts

3 things I like about . . .	
2 concerns I have . . .	
1 idea I'd like to explore . . .	

Figure 71   Choice board for study of World War II

1 Design four posters using your own drawings or pictures that depict the characteristics of life during World War II. Use captions to explain your visuals.	**2** Develop an interview questionnaire; then interview at least four people who lived in this area during World War II. Describe at last five ways the war affected their lives.	**3** Write and present a short one-act play that depicts life during World War II, either at home or overseas. Use support material from novels or historical references.
4 Read a book, such as *The Diary of Anne Frank,* and briefly describe four scenarios from the story showing how World War II changed the characters' lives.	**5** Wild Card! Your choice. Please design an option and present it in writing by _____.	**6** Produce a PowerPoint presentation using visuals, scripts, and sound to show life as one would have experienced it during World War II.
7 Listen to a variety of songs, musicals, and film soundtracks composed during World War II. Referring to the content of the songs, describe what the music conveys about what life was like during the war.	**8** Collect a variety of pictures, newspaper articles, photographs, poems, and stories. Noting aspects of life during World War II, create a personal diary of how you would have felt growing up in that time.	**9** Create a board game designed to increase understanding of what life was like during World War II.

Teacher direction: Put a choice in each box. Use as many boxes as needed. There should be more lines on the total choice board than there are students in the classroom. This gives the last group a chance to have a selection.

Student direction: Sign up for the one you choose.

Figure 72   Planning template for Eight Choices plus a wild card for any unit of study

---

Unit on _____

Choose one of the following options as a culminating activity for this unit

1	2	3
Design six posters using your own drawings or pictures that depict the characteristics _____ _____. Use captions to explain your visuals.	Develop an interview questionnaire, then interview at least four people who _____. Describe at least five ways _____	Write and present a short one-act play that depicts _____. Use support material from _____
4	**5**	**6**
Read _____ and briefly describe four different scenarios from _____ showing _____	Wild Card! Your choice. Please design an option and present it in writing by _____	Produce a PowerPoint presentation using visuals, scripts, and sound to present _____
7	**8**	**9**
Listen to a variety of songs, musicals, or create a song to the tune of _____	Collect a variety of pictures newspaper articles, photographs, poems, and stories.	Design a board game to increase understanding of _____

Figure 73 Differentiation review for faculty meeting or study group activity

Differentiation: A Review

Find a colleague who can . . .

1. Explain why you think differentiation is important in today's classrooms.	2. Tell what part multiple intelligence plays in your planning for differentiation.	3. Define focus activities and describe examples that you use in your classroom.
4. Explain how relaxed alertness is possible in a differentiated classroom.	5. Define cubing and give an example of how you might use it.	6. Tell how a teacher's role changes in a differentiated classroom.
7. Complete the statement, "A differentiated classroom is like a _____ because _____."	8. Share your thoughts about compacting.	9. Tell one thing that you can do to reach the diverse learners in your classroom.

■ REFLECTIONS

1. Discuss and share the curriculum models you have used successfully in your classroom.

2. Share some personal tips and variations that helped you be successful using the following:

   Centers

   Projects

   Choice boards

   Problem-based learning

   Contracts

II-8

Putting It All Together in Your Differentiated Classroom

After teachers have explored all the elements of differentiation offered throughout this book, they may want to review the planning templates (Figures 75, and 76). Teachers may examine the lesson plan examples in Chapter 3 (Figures 5.7 and 5.9) and Chapter 8 (Figures 8.2 and 8.3) of *Differentiated Instructional Strategies: One Size Doesn't Fit All* (3rd ed.; Gregory & Chapman, 2013) and identify the ways the teacher has differentiated (readiness, interest, multiple intelligence, process). Another discussion might be how else that standard could have been attained. What other methods or strategies could have been used? What other types of differentiated instruction could have been used?

Figure 74   The six-step planning model for differentiated learning: template

Planning for Differentiated Learning	
1. **STANDARDS:** What should students know and be able to do?	Assessment tools for data collection (logs, checklists, journals, agendas, observations, portfolios, rubrics, contracts)
Essential Questions:	
2. **CONTENT:** (concepts, vocabulary, facts)	**SKILLS**
3. **ACTIVATE:** Focus Activity: Pre-assessment strategy Pre-assessment Prior knowledge and engaging the learners	• Quiz, test • Surveys • K-W-L • Journals • Arm gauge • Give me • Brainstorm • Concept formation • Thumb it
4. **ACQUIRE:** Total group or small groups	• Lecturette • Presentation • Demonstration • Jigsaw • Video • Field trip • Guest speaker • Text
5. **Grouping Decisions:** TAPS, random, heterogeneous, homogeneous, interest, task, constructed **APPLY** **ADJUST**	• Learning centers • Projects • Contracts • Compact/Enrichment • Problem based • Inquiry • Research • Independent study
6. **ASSESS** Diversity honored (learning styles, multiple intelligences, personal interest, etc.)	• Quiz, test • Performance • Products • Presentation • Demonstration • Log, journal • Checklist • Portfolio • Rubric • Metacognition

Figure 75   Planning for differentiated learning for middle school science: Exploring the functions of the body's skeletal and muscular systems

Planning for Differentiated Learning	
1. STANDARDS: What should students know and be able to do? Skeletal and muscular systems work together to carry out the life function of locomotion.	Assessment tools for data collection (logs, checklists, journals, agendas, observations, portfolios, rubrics, contracts)
Essential Questions: What functions do skeletal and muscular systems provide? How do we better care for these systems?	
2. CONTENT: (concepts, vocabulary, facts) Muscles, skeleton, functions, ligaments, bones	**SKILLS:** Visual representations, cause and effect
3. ACTIVATE: Focus Activity: Pre-assessment strategy Pre-assessment Prior knowledge and engaging the learners 3 Functions of skeletal/muscular system 2 Questions you would like to ask 1 Reason this is good to know Label the parts of the skeletal and muscular systems	• Quiz, test • Surveys • K-W-L • Journals • Arm gauge • Give me • Brainstorm • Concept formation • Thumb it
4. ACQUIRE: Total group or small groups View video in groups of three with an advanced organizer. Small-group discussion and fill-in advance organizer as a summarizing and note-taking piece. Compare information from video with textbook reading working with a random partner.	• Lecturette • Presentation • Demonstration • Jigsaw • Video • Field trip • Guest speaker • Text
5. Grouping Decisions: TAPS, random, heterogeneous, homogeneous, interest, task, constructed **APPLY** **ADJUST** Students will group according to the choices they make from the choice board. Students will work alone, in pairs, or in trios to complete two projects on the choice board. Students will present their projects from the choice board. Teacher and peers provide feedback with rubric.	• Learning centers • Projects • Contracts • Compact/enrichment • Problem based • Inquiry • Research • Independent study
6. ASSESS Students will individually write a paper on the necessity and functions of the skeletal and muscular systems and their efforts to take care of these systems for healthy living. Test on parts and functions of the two systems. Diversity honored (learning styles, multiple intelligences, personal interest, etc.)	• Quiz, test • Performance • Products • Presentation • Demonstration • Log, journal • Checklist • Portfolio • Rubric • Metacognition

Figure 76   Planning for differentiated learning for high school social studies: Examining the impact of European immigrant on American culture

Planning for Differentiated Learning	
1. STANDARDS: What should students know and be able to do? Examine the influx of European immigrants and their contributions to American society.	Assessment tools for data collection (logs, checklists, journals, agendas, observations, portfolios, rubrics, contracts)
Essential Questions: How has the ethnicity of immigrants in the early 21st century influenced and affected our lives in the United States?	
2. CONTENT: (concepts, vocabulary, facts) Immigration, culture, emigration, relocation, ethnicity, employment, religion	**SKILLS:** Compare and contrast, research and data collection, visual representation
3. ACTIVATE: Focus Activity: Pre-assessment strategy Pre-assessment Prior knowledge and engaging the learners Students create a four-corner organizer to fill in what they know about immigration at the beginning of the 21st century. Each student will generate a personal question. Guest speaker: immigrant grandparent.	• Quiz, test • Surveys • K-W-L • Journals • Arm gauge • Give me • Brainstorm • Concept formation • Thumb it
4. ACQUIRE: Total group or small groups From an interest survey, students will identify which groups of immigrants they would like to investigate more thoroughly. Students will use the Internet, text, resource center, and community resources to gather information on a W5 chart.	• Lecturette • Presentation • Demonstration • Jigsaw • Video • Field trip • Guest speaker • Text
5. Grouping Decisions: TAPS, random, heterogeneous, homogeneous, interest, task, constructed **APPLY** **ADJUST** Students in small groups will present their findings to the total class. Each student will partner with another student who investigated a different ethnicity of immigrants using a cross-classification matrix. Students will regroup until the entire chart is filled in and all students have discussed all immigrant groups.	• Learning centers • Projects • Contracts • Compact/enrichment • Problem based • Inquiry • Research • Independent study
6. ASSESS Students will create a mind map in small groups to symbolize the contributions of immigrants to the American culture. Test on immigration in the early 21st century and the impact of the different ethnic groups. Diversity honored (learning styles, multiple intelligences, personal interest, etc.)	• Quiz, test • Performance • Products • Presentation • Demonstration • Log, journal • Checklist • Portfolio • Rubric • Metacognition

Part III

Managing Change in the Professional Learning Community

III-1

The Implementation Process

FACING A CHANGE IN PRACTICE ■

In *Taking Charge of Change,* Hord, Rutherford, Huling-Austin, and Hall (1987) suggest that there are several stages of concern educators have when they are facing a change in practice of the kind involved in differentiated instruction. The discussion of the following stages has been adapted from their Concerns-Based Adoption Model:

- *Non-use*, including awareness and information: Teachers usually don't know about the innovation and are not practicing it in the classroom due to lack of awareness or information.
- *Early Use*, including personal and management concerns: As teachers begin to use differentiated instruction, they have concerns about their personal efficacy and performance and about their ability to manage the classroom proceedings.
- *Maturing Use*, including consequences and collaboration: Teachers with maturing abilities in the classroom begin to look beyond their own concerns. They start to consider the impact the innovation is having on students and their successes and how sharing their ideas with colleagues can impact student learning.
- *Mastery*, including refocusing: At this point teachers are reflective and evaluative concerning the process of differentiation. They are now often able to "find a better way" through adjusting and experimenting with other strategies.

Often, in our attempt to implement new ideas, we rush to in-service training and workshops, when in reality people need opportunities to dialogue about the concept and develop a shared vision of how the innovation would look and sound in their classroom and in their school. Figure 77 lists some of the issues faced during implementation and offers ideas for responding to these issues. Administrators and teachers may want to examine this chart and identify the support teachers might find useful at each stage of concern.

■ ADOPTER TYPES AND CHANGE

Everett Rogers (1995) and others have studied how an innovation diffuses through a group of people. People differ in their readiness to accept change. Some adopt new ideas quickly and run with them, while others take a longer time. Figure 78 describes the various categories of adopter types and suggests the different kinds of support each group needs.

Administrators may want to identify (without labeling) where people on the faculty are in terms of adopter types and look at focusing on the Innovators and Leaders who are ready, able, and open to differentiation. That is not to say that we won't worry about the Late Majority and Resistors, but we have only so much time, energy, and resources, so we had better put them where they will have the most impact and influence. To use a gardening metaphor, "Don't water the rocks, water the flowers."

If we can engage the first three groups (Innovators, Leaders, and Early Majority), we have the potential to create a critical mass of implementers (52%) who will create a momentum that may engage those (Late Majority and Resistors) who have been less interested in differentiation. Continuing to engage the Resistors in dialogue may increase our awareness of where their concerns lie and may help us help them begin the implementation journey. As Maurer (1996) suggests, we may want to walk toward the resistance so that we can better understand the reasons for and concerns about the change. Often, Resistors have seen too many innovations come and go, initiated but not really implemented, and they may have become naturally skeptical about "this year's new thing."

A strategy for breaking down barriers that could be used at a faculty meeting is to have a reverse debate. Ask half the faculty (divide the room with an invisible line) to brainstorm all the reasons that we should try differentiating instruction and how it might work. Invite the other half to generate all the aspects that would be negative and why differentiation wouldn't work. Then ask the groups to switch positions and brainstorm again. This is a way to legitimize the naysayers and also solve problems around some of the genuine concerns and barriers up front.

■ THE PROCESS OF CHANGE

We know that change is personal, both emotional and cognitive in nature, and even if we embrace the change, emotions will be part of the context of our process. Ken Blanchard (1983) reminds us that when people find themselves experiencing change, they often react in predictable ways. Figure 79

Figure 77   Faculty concerns about differentiated instruction

It is very important to listen to and recognize what concerns people have about differentiation and give them what they need to satisfy their concerns.

Stages of Concern	Expressions of Concerns	Support for Differentiation
Mastery *Refocusing* I have some ideas about something that would work even better. *Collaboration* How can I relate what I am doing to what others are doing?	I've tried _____ and I'd like to do _____ differently. Maybe we could _____ . A variation of _____ might be _____ . I'd like to work with _____ to refine _____ .	Help individuals access the resources they may need to refine their ideas and put them into practice. Respect the interest they may have in "finding a better way" (Hord et al., 1987). Develop opportunities for individuals to use the innovation collaboratively or to discuss applications of the innovation in collaborative settings.
Maturing Use *Consequence* How is this affecting other processes?	What difference is all this making to my students' learning? I don't want students to feel like "buzzards and bluebirds" when I use flexible grouping. Has the climate in my classroom changed? How are students feeling?	Provide individuals with opportunities to visit other settings where the innovation is in use and to share their skills with others. Continue to provide positive feedback and support.
Early Use *Management* I seem to be spending all my time on getting materials and learning new skills. *Personal* How will the new approach or process affect me?	How do I manage all these groups? Sometimes it feels like a three-ring circus. What if I lose control? I don't feel comfortable or capable sometimes. I don't have time for all the planning that this takes.	Provide help with the small, specific how-to issues that are often the cause of management concerns. Offer assistance with the logistical problems that lead to these concerns. Make sure individuals know that others share their concerns. Provide support and encouragement. Reinforce a sense of personal adequacy. Put individuals in contact with others who have managed the change successfully. Make it seem doable, bit by bit.
Non-use *Informational* I would like to know more about it. *Non-awareness* I am not concerned about it.	I don't understand this! Don't we already do this? I need more information. What do other teachers who are differentiating say and feel? Oh, great! This month's new thing. I've seen this before. This too shall pass.	Use a variety of methods for sharing information. Communicate with individuals and with large and small groups. Have persons who have used the new process in other settings talk with your group. Share enough information to arouse interest, but not so much that it overwhelms.

Figure 78   Adopter types and support needed

Types	Support Suggested
Innovators (8%) Eager to try ideas, open to change, willing to take risks. Usually perceived as naïve and a little crazy and not well integrated into staff.	They need vision and support, encouragement and help with resources and materials. They need protection from the naysayers while they experiment. They need opportunities to further investigate the topic and attend workshops and conferences.
Leaders (17%) Open to change, but more thoughtful about getting involved. Trusted by staff and sought for advice and opinions.	They need articles and research that support the innovation. They need visits to classrooms where it is working. Perhaps book study and video presentations would be helpful for examination and reflection.
Early Majority (29%) Cautious and deliberate about deciding to adopt an innovation. Tend to be followers, not leaders.	Partner them with leaders. Have innovators and leaders share ideas at faculty meetings. Provide time to collaborate and visit with others.
Late Majority (29%) Skeptical of adopting new ideas; set in their ways. Can be won over by peer pressure and administrative expectations.	Partner them with people in the early majority group who are not too intimidating or zealous. Encourage peer planning, coaching, and teaching. Help them set manageable, attainable goals.
Resistors (17%) Suspicious and generally opposed to new ideas. Usually low in influence and often isolated from the mainstream.	Keep them informed. Give them every opportunity to become involved at any point. Listen to their resistance, and investigate their point of view. Share staff, student, and perhaps parent testimonials. Set expectations through the supervision process. Provide pressure and support!

lists some of the emotions and feelings experienced by those who face change along with supportive responses.

■ THE IMPLEMENTATION DIP

Even though we try to set up conditions that support and encourage change, it is still inevitable that we'll meet stumbling blocks along the way. Michael Fullan (1991, 2001) and others refer to this as the *implementation dip*.

The implementation process generally begins with enthusiasm and confidence. However, people sometimes lose momentum or meet obstacles

Figure 79   Emotional aspects of adjusting to change

Feelings as People Face Change	Supportive Responses
Feel self-conscious and awkward when they are asked to do something new.	Give people support and time to try new strategies until they feel more comfortable.
Grieve for what they have to give up.	Have a symbolic burial for the old ways.
Feel alone, even though others are changing, too.	Facilitate opportunities for colleagues to problem-solve and dialogue as well as share strategies.
Feel overwhelmed at the complexity of the change.	Help people "bite off" manageable tasks that can be accomplished.
Are at different levels of readiness for the change.	Listen to concerns and support, and encourage people with what they need at any point in time.
Concerned that they won't have the resources that they will need.	Help people find the resources they need, and provide what is necessary to move them forward in implementation.
Revert back to their old ways if the pressure is removed.	Keep people focused on the innovation by supplying the needed pressure and support.

and challenges that slow down their progress or cause them to give up. All innovations will present problems during implementation, but the trick is to recognize the implementation dip and collaborate to solve problems and seek solutions that will help sustain the progress.

One creative principal organized a "dip party" when he recognized that people were experiencing an implementation dip. People brought their favorite snacks and dips and problem-solved together to raise spirits and buoy renewed energy to continue "working on the work." See also Gregory and Kuzmich's (2007) *Teacher Teams That Work* for more strategies for sustaining learning communities as they tackle deep implementation.

III-2

Observation and Supervision

Encouragement and support are needed during the process of implementation. Evaluation should come later when teachers are further along in the process.

PRESSURE, SUPPORT, AND EVALUATION DURING IMPLEMENTATION ■

Saphier and King (1985) suggest that there are 12 cultural norms that support growth in a positive culture:

1. Collegiality
2. Experimentation
3. High expectations
4. Trust and confidence
5. Tangible support
6. Reaching out to the knowledge base
7. Appreciation and recognition
8. Caring, celebration, and humor
9. Involvement in decision making
10. Protection of what is important
11. Traditions
12. Honest, open communication

Principals who adopt these norms can support the creation and development of a positive culture for learning for adults and, ultimately, for students.

Seven Steps to Keeping Up Morale During Implementation

Step 1. Be vigilant in finding things that can be celebrated. Leave notes in teacher mailboxes whenever you see an attempt at differentiating and meeting student needs.

Step 2. Recognize any gains and be sensitive when a teacher is frustrated or disheartened. Perhaps plan a "dip party" when an implementation dip is encountered.

Step 3. Publish successes in a weekly newsletter, post an accomplishment on the faculty room bulletin board, and/or honor teachers during each staff meeting.

Step 4. Collect comments from students about their reactions to differentiated tasks, and use them to thank teachers.

Step 5. Present a certificate of effort or attendance at study groups or for staff meeting sharing.

Step 6. Offer to take over a class or a duty so that teachers have an extended planning opportunity or may visit another classroom or school.

Step 7. Offer resources to help and encourage teachers to try something new.

■ "WALKABOUTS"

As instructional leaders, principals need to be seen as knowledgeable about differentiation. They need to develop a shared vision and language with the faculty. Principals who are visible daily in classrooms heighten teachers' awareness of quality instruction and provide recognition and encouragement during the implementation of innovations.

Management by walking or wandering is another extremely effective way to both monitor instructional and assessment practices and open doors to dialogue with teachers. It helps to deprivatize the teaching process, and it lowers teachers' anxiety through informal interactions about student learning. A powerful video produced by McREL titled *Principles in Action* (http://www.youtube.com/watch?v=AdOuWt6cfW0) features several effective faculties and their collaborative work in improving student learning. One example is Debbie Backus, in Aurora, Colorado, who shows her vigilance in focusing on student learning daily through interactions with teachers, students, and parents.

These informal visits and walkabouts help principals get a daily read on the following:

- Classroom climate
- Learners' knowledge

- Instructional and assessment practices in the school
- Professionalism of faculty

During the walkabouts, principals can enhance positive aspects of classroom practices by commenting verbally, leaving brief notes for the teacher, or sharing best practices noticed during the week at a faculty meeting. This is an opportunity to honor heroes, heroines, and risk takers who are trying differentiated instruction. Everyone likes to be recognized, and it isn't long before word spreads about what gets noticed and celebrated.

Administrators may also inquire of teachers whether they would like feedback or data on some aspect of instruction or assessment that they are trying to implement, or data about a challenging student they are trying to reach. Data presented as information for the teacher to reflect on, respond to, or use for problem solving increases interaction with trusted colleagues.

Principals may want to tell the staff about the walkabouts and why they are important to the principal, the faculty, and the school as a whole. There may also be a specific focus for the month, for example: How is flexible grouping being used? Adjustable assignments? Evidence of a positive climate?

SEVEN WAYS TO FIND TIME

Time, of course, is always a scarce resource in schools, and administrators need to be creative in finding ways to help teachers collaborate with colleagues and implement new innovations. Many principals are quite creative in how they find time for teachers to collaborate and discuss their craft. Here are seven methods for finding more time:

1. *"Bank" time:* Some schools bank time by adding a few minutes a day to the schedule and accumulating a block of time for collaboration by releasing students early or beginning classes later one morning every few weeks.

2. *Early release:* Other districts have established an early release format; each Wednesday afternoon students are released at 2:30 p.m. so that teachers can plan between then and 4:30 p.m.

3. *Buddy system:* Teachers can develop a buddy system for their students, teaming them with students from another grade level, so that when the two students meet one teacher can monitor the buddies and the other teacher can meet with his or her planning partner.

4. *"Grandparent" program:* Some schools have a grandparent program. This means that retired qualified teachers and administrators volunteer their time one or two afternoons a month in order to allow teachers to plan collaboratively.

5. *Community service:* Many secondary programs require students to engage in community service. If that community service can be coordinated so that students are all participating at the same time, then teachers can be freed to collaborate and plan for differentiation.

6. *Morning meetings:* If there is a high level of commitment, teachers may agree to meet for an hour or so before school starts once a week to plan and share ideas. (See also Bagel Breakfast in Chapter I-2.)

7. *Summer break:* Many schools with committed teachers also take advantage of summertime, when teachers can participate in workshops or summer institutes, work on curriculum to embed differentiation, or team plan. This is a good time for teachers to focus without the worry of leaving their students or planning for a substitute teacher.

Some districts offer professional development credits toward recertification or graduate work. If possible, stipends may be given for extra time. This is a very good way to get the "keen teachers" trained to be a cadre of support and a resource for the school.

■ IDENTIFYING KNOWLEDGE AND SKILLS NEEDED

Teachers are more comfortable with any innovation if they are clear about the *what* and the *how* of the innovation and the benefits it will have for students if it is implemented. In facilitating change, we have to be clear about the knowledge and skills that teachers need in order to be successful in differentiating instruction for and with students.

Teachers Should Know

- Facts: Define differentiation and its importance (rationale)
- Common language: Content, readiness, process (activities), interest, products, learning styles, multiple intelligences
- Expectations:

    – Students are given respectful tasks.

    – Students are grouped flexibly.

    – Students are offered varied instructional strategies.

    – Students are given choices.

Teachers Should Understand

- All students are unique, and they learn in different ways on different days.
- Teachers are responsible for engaging and coaching students and providing high-quality interactions, materials, and environments within a clearly focused curriculum.

Teachers Should Be Able to Create the Following Learning Opportunities

- Target standards
- Offer relevant and meaningful tasks to students

- Encourage creativity
- Develop skills
- Allow for student choices

IMPLEMENTATION PROFILE ■

An implementation profile is very similar to a rubric, and we know how helpful rubrics are in keeping a target visible and attainable when we persist and take small steps toward continuous improvement. The profile provides four levels of implementation: Non-use (mechanical), Beginning, Routine, and Refined (Figure 80). It is a continuum that administrators and teachers can use as a conversation piece to assess where they are in terms of each of the areas outlined as necessary for differentiated instruction. The profile helps faculty members know where they are and set goals for continued growth in the areas that are targeted for further improvement.

EVALUATION AND REFLECTION ■

Principals and administrators need to collect data during their observations and walkabouts so that a dialogue may take place with teachers to encourage reflection and to identify areas of strength and opportunities for growth. Figure 81 may be useful for collecting data in various categories.

Cognitive coaching strategies (Costa & Garmston, 2002) can be useful in sharing the data and encouraging faculty to reflect, project, and solve problems in response to the data. Figure 82 may also be used as a reflection tool for teachers. Its checklist of questions for planning differentiated learning will be useful as teachers begin to move toward more differentiated classrooms. It can help them measure their progress from time to time as they implement their new ideas and strategies.

The strategies, ideas, and templates in this book are designed to assist teachers and administrators as they work collaboratively to explore, examine, and implement differentiated instruction to better serve their students. This is a journey of self-examination and discovery, not a quick fix to learning. It is also not a panacea for the struggles that each teacher faces as she or he responds to a group of 20, 30, or more individuals in classrooms each day.

David Perkins (1995) reminds us that intelligence consists of a combination of deep knowledge within multiple domains, the ability to recognize patterns, the ability to consciously access a variety of strategies, and thoughtful reflection. As professionals, teachers should be constantly honing their craft with both the art and science of teaching in order to respond with intelligent behavior to learners' needs so that all may succeed.

Figure 80   Implementation profile

	Non-use	Beginning	Routine	Refined
Creating the Climate	Restrictive Lacking warmth or student focus	Warm Engaging Openness Safe	Warm/fun Engaging Openness Supportive Safe Inclusive Enthusiastic Responsive	Student are in "flow" Responsive individually and collectively Encouraging risk taking Questioning Cubing
Knowing the Learner	No attempt made to identify uniqueness of the learner	Students' learning styles and multiple intelligences are explored	Teacher provides a variety of instructional and assessment practices to routinely respect styles and multiple intelligences of students	Through reflection and conferences with students, teacher builds on and sets goals with students, considering their uniqueness
Assessing the Learner	Test at the end of a unit	Consideration of standards and objectives Attempts are made to pre-assess using several methods of data collection Test or presentation	Consideration of standards Pre-assessment for planning purposes Specific data collection methods based on expectations Choice of evaluation, presentation, or activity to demonstrate knowledge and skills	Consideration of standards Pre-assessment for planning purposes Specific data collection methods based on expectations Choice of evaluation, presentation, or activity to demonstrate knowledge and skills Students use peer and self-assessment techniques
Adjusting Assignments	One lesson for all Total groups	Teacher groups students for a variety of activities	Teacher uses a variety of flexible groups: heterogeneous and homogenous	Teacher uses appropriate groupings: total, alone, pairs, small groups, heterogeneous, and homogeneous
Brain-Compatible Instruction	Mostly "sit and get" One size fits all	Teacher uses instruction based on personal repertoire	Teacher selects instructional strategies that are research based/best practices and continues to increase personal repertoire	Teacher uses research-based, brain-compatible strategies appropriate to the learner and content, recognizing students' learning styles and multiple intelligences
Curriculum Models	Mostly teacher-directed lessons All students doing the same thing	Teacher uses some projects and problems More student centered	Teacher uses problems, inquiry, centers, and contracts as appropriate	Students have input into the design of curriculum Teacher considers all models and their appropriateness for grouping, learning styles, and multiple intelligences

Figure 81   Differentiation: Elements for planning observation

Climate	Knowing the Learner	Assessing the Learner	Adjustable Assignments	Instructional Strategies	Curriculum Approaches
• Safe	Learning profiles	Pre-assessment	Compacting	Brain/research based	Centers
• Nurturing		*Before*		Memory model	
• Encourages risk taking		• Formal		Elaborative rehearsal	
• Inclusive	Multiple intelligences		Gifted	Focus activities	Projects
• Multisensory		• Informal		Graphic organizers	
• Stimulating				Metaphors	
• Complex	Culture		TAPS	Cooperative group learning	
• Challenging		*During*	*Total group*	Jigsaw	Problem-based learning
• Collaborative	Gender	• Formal		Questioning	
• Team and class building			*Alone*	Cubing	
• Norms	Pop culture	• Informal		Role-play	Inquiry
• Mindset			*Paired*	Technology	
		After			
		• Formal	*Small groups*		Contracts
		• Informal			

Figure 82   Checklist of questions for teachers planning differentiated learning for their students

uilding Safe Environments

- Do students feel safe to risk and experiment with ideas?
- Do students feel included in the class and supported by others?
- Are tasks challenging enough without undo or "dis" stress?
- Is there an emotional "hook" for the learners?
- Are there novel, unique, and engaging activities to capture and sustain attention?
- Are "unique brains" honored and provided for? (learning styles & multiple intelligences)

ecognizing and Honoring Diversity

- Does the learning experience appeal to the learners' varied and multiple intelligences and learning styles?
- May the students work collaboratively and independently?
- May they "show what they know" in a variety of ways?
- Does the cultural background of the learners influence instruction?

ssessment

- Are pre-assessments given to determine readiness?
- Is there enough time to explore, understand, and transfer the learning to long-term memory (grow dendrites)? Is there time to accomplish mastery?
- Do they have opportunities for ongoing, "just in time" feedback?
- Do they have time to revisit ideas and concepts to connect or extend them?
- Is metacognitive time built into the learning process?
- Do students use logs and journals for reflection and goal setting?

nstructional Strategies

- Are the expectations clearly stated and understood by the learner?
- Will the learning be relevant and useful to the learner?
- Does the learning build on past experience or create a new experience?
- Does the learning relate to their real world?
- Are strategies developmentally appropriate and hands-on?
- Are the strategies varied to engage and sustain attention?
- Are there opportunities for projects, creativity, problems, and challenges?

umerous Curriculum Approaches

- Do students work alone, in pairs, and in small groups?
- Do students work in learning centers based on interest, need, or choice?
- Are some activities adjusted to provide appropriate levels of challenge?
- Is pretesting used to allow for compacting/enrichment?
- Are problems, inquiries, and contracts considered?

Training Resources

BOOKS ■

Cole, D. J., Ryan, C. W., Kick, F., & Mathies, B. K. (2000). *Portfolios across the curriculum and beyond* (2nd ed.). Thousand Oaks, CA: Corwin.

Gregory, G. H., & Chapman, C. (2013). *Differentiated instructional strategies: One size doesn't fit all* (3rd ed.). Thousand Oaks, CA: Corwin.

Rolheiser, C., Bower, B., & Stevahn, L. (2000). *The portfolio organizer: Succeeding with portfolios in your classroom.* Alexandria, VA: Association for Supervision and Curriculum Development.

Tomlinson, C. A. (1998a). *Differentiating instruction: Facilitator's guide.* Alexandria, VA: Association for Supervision and Curriculum Development.

VIDEOS ■

Gregory, G. H., & Chapman, C. (2002a). *Differentiating instruction to meet the needs of all learners: Elementary edition.* Sandy, UT: Teach Stream/Video Journal of Education.

Gregory, G. H., & Chapman, C. (2002b). *Differentiating instruction to meet the needs of all learners: Secondary edition.* Sandy, UT: Teach Stream/Video Journal of Education.

McREL. (2000). *Principles in action: Stories of award-winning professional development.* Aurora, CO: McREL.

Tomlinson, C. A. (1998b). *Differentiating instruction: Tape 2: Instructional and Management Strategies.* Alexandria, VA: Association for Supervision and Curriculum Development.

WEB SITE ■

RubiStar. Web site that helps teachers create rubrics for project-based learning activities. http://rubistar.4teachers.org

Bibliography

Aronson, E. (1978). *The jigsaw classroom.* Thousand Oaks, CA: Sage.

Bennett, B., Rolheiser-Bennett, C., & Stevahn, L. (1991). *Cooperative learning: Where heart meets mind.* Toronto, Ontario, Canada: Educational Connections.

Bellanca, J., & Fogarty, R. (1991). *Blueprints for thinking in the cooperative classroom.* Thousand Oaks, CA: Corwin.

Blanchard, K. H. (1983). *The one minute manager.* New York, NY: Berkley.

Bloom, B. S. (Ed). (1956). Taxonomy of educational objectives. *Handbook 1: Cognitive domain.* New York, NY: Longman, Green.

Cole, D. J., Ryan, C. W., Kick, F., & Mathies, B. K. (2000). *Portfolios across the curriculum and beyond* (2nd ed.). Thousand Oaks, CA: Corwin.

Collins, D. (1998). *Achieving your vision of professional development.* Greensboro, NC: SERVE.

Costa, A., & Garmston, R. (2002). *Cognitive coaching: A foundation for Renaissance Schools* (2nd ed.). Norwood, MA: Christopher-Gordon.

de Bono, E. (1987). *Edward de Bono's CoRT Thinking.* Boston, MA: Advanced Practical Thinking.

de Bono, E. (1999). *Six thinking hats.* Boston, MA: Back Bay Books.

Deal, T. E., & Peterson, K. D. (1999). *Shaping school culture: The heart of leadership.* San Francisco, CA: Jossey-Bass.

DuFour, R., & Eaker, R. (1998). *Professional learning communities at work: Best practices for enhancing student achievement.* Bloomington, IN: National Educational Service.

Dunn, R., & Dunn, K. (1987). Dispelling outmoded beliefs about student learning. *Educational Leadership, 44*(6), 55–61.

Easton, L. B. (Ed.). (2004). *Powerful designs for professional learning.* Oxford, OH: National Staff Development Council.

Fogarty, R., & Stoehr, J. (1995). Integrating curricula with multiple intelligences: *Teams, themes, and threads.* Thousand Oaks, CA: Corwin.

Fullan, M. (with Steigelbauer, S.). (1991). *The new meaning of educational change.* New York, NY: Teachers College Press.

Fullan, M. (2001). *Leading in a culture of change.* San Francisco, CA: Jossey-Bass.

Gardner, H. (1983). *Frames of mind: The theory of multiple intelligences.* New York, NY: Basic Books.

Gardner, H. (1993). *Multiple intelligences: The theory in practice.* New York, NY: Basic Books.

Glasser, W. (1990). *The quality school.* New York, NY: Harper & Row.

Goleman, D. (1995). *Emotional intelligence.* New York, NY: Bantam.

Goleman, D. (1998). *Working with emotional intelligence.* New York, NY: Bantam.

Gregorc, A. (1982). *Inside styles: Beyond the basics.* Columbia, CT: Gregorc Associates.

Gregory, G. H. (2005). *Differentiating instruction with style.* Thousand Oaks, CA: Corwin.

Gregory, G. H., & Chapman, C. (2002a). *Differentiating instruction to meet the needs of all learners: Elementary edition.* Sandy, UT: Teach Stream/Video Journal of Education.

Gregory, G. H., & Chapman, C. (2002b). *Differentiating instruction to meet the needs of all learners: Secondary edition.* Sandy, UT: Teach Stream/Video Journal of Education.

Gregory, G. H., & Chapman, C. M. (2007). *Differentiated instructional strategies: One size doesn't fit all* (2nd ed.). Thousand Oaks, CA: Corwin.

Gregory, G. H., & Chapman, C. M. (2013). *Differentiated instructional strategies: One size doesn't fit all* (3rd ed.). Thousand Oaks, CA: Corwin.

Gregory, G. H., & Kuzmich, L. (2007). *Teacher teams that work.* Thousand Oaks, CA: Corwin.

Gregory, G., & Parry, T. (2006). *Designing brain-compatible learning* (3rd ed.). Thousand Oaks, CA: Corwin.

Guskey, T. R. (1994). Teacher efficacy: A study of construct dimensions. *American Educational Research Journal, 31,* 627–641.

Hord, S., Rutherford, W. L., Huling-Austin, L., & Hall, G. E. (1987). *Taking charge of change.* Alexandria, VA: Association of Supervision and Curriculum Development.

Joyce, B., & Showers, B. (1995). *Student achievement through staff development: Fundamentals of school renewal.* New York, NY: Longman.

Kagan, S. (1992). *Cooperative learning.* San Clemente, CA: Kagan.

Kohn, A. (1993). *Punished by rewards.* Boston, MA: Houghton Mifflin.

Kolb, D. (1984). *Experiential learning: Experience as the source of learning and development.* Englewood Cliffs, NJ: Prentice Hall.

Maslow, A. (1954). *Motivation and personality.* New York, NY: Harper & Row.

Maslow, A. (1968). *Toward a psychology of being.* New York, NY: Van Nostrand Reinhold.

Maurer, R. (1996). *Beyond the wall of resistance.* Austin, TX: Bard Books.

Ministry of Education. (1979). *Research study skills: Curriculum ideas for teachers.* Toronto, Ontario, Canada: Author.

Murphy, C. U., & Lick, D. W. (2001). *Whole-faculty study groups: Creating student-based professional development.* Thousand Oaks, CA: Corwin.

Newmann, F., King, B., & Youngs, P. (2000). *Professional development that addresses school capacity: Lessons from urban elementary schools.* Paper presented at the annual conference of the American Educational Research Association.

Perkins, D. (1995). *Outsmarting IQ: The emerging science of learnable intelligence.* New York, NY: Free Press.

Robbins, P., Gregory, G., & Herndon, L. (2000). *Thinking inside the block schedule.* Thousand Oaks, CA: Corwin.

Rogers, E. M. (1995). *Diffusion of innovations* (4th ed.). New York, NY: Free Press.

Rolheiser, C., Bower, B., & Stevahn, L. (2000). *The portfolio organizer: Succeeding with portfolios in your classroom.* Alexandria, VA: Association for Supervision and Curriculum Development.

Sagor, R. (1992). *How to conduct collaborative action research.* Alexandria, VA: Association for Supervision and Curriculum Development.

Saphier, J., & King, M. (1985). Good seeds grow in strong cultures. *Educational Leadership, 38,* 66–77.

Senge, P. M. (1990). *The fifth discipline: The art and practice of the learning organization.* New York, NY: Doubleday.

Slavin, R. E. (1994). *Cooperative learning: Theory, research, and practice.* Boston, MA: Allyn & Bacon.

Sparks, D., & Hirsh, S. (1997). *A new vision for staff development.* Alexandria, VA: Association for Supervision and Curriculum Development.

Sternberg, R. (1996). *Successful intelligence: How practical and creative intelligence determine success in life.* New York, NY: Simon & Schuster.

Taba, H. (1962). *Curriculum development: Theory and practice.* Washington, DC: International Thomson.

Taba, H. (1999). *The dynamics of education: A methodology of progressive educational thought.* New York, NY: Routledge.

Tomlinson, C. A. (1998b). *Differentiating instruction: Tape 2: Instructional and management strategies.* Alexandria, VA: Association for Supervision and Curriculum Development.

SUGGESTED READINGS ◼

Anderson, L., & Krathwohl, D. (Eds.). (2001). *A taxonomy for learning, teaching, and assessing: A revision of Bloom's taxonomy of educational objectives.* New York, NY: Addison-Wesley Longman.

Black, P., Harrison, C., Lee, C., Marshall, B., & Wiliam, D. (2004). Working inside the black box: Assessment for learning in the classroom. *Phi Delta Kappan, 86*(1), 9–21.

Black, P., & Wiliam, D. (2009). Developing the theory of formative assessment. *Educational Assessment, Evaluation, and Accountability, 21,* 5–31.

Brain, M. (2000). *How laughter works.* Retrieved from http://health.howstuffworks.com/mental-health/human-nature/other-emotions/laughter.htm

Dean, C. B., Hubbell, E. R., Pitler, H., & Stone, B. J. (2012). Classroom instruction that works: Research-based strategies for increasing student achievement (2nd ed.). Alexandria, VA. Association for Supervision and Curriculum Development.

Diamond, M. (2001). Response of the brain to enrichment. *Annals of the Brazilian Academy of Sciences, 73,* 61.

Dweck, C. S. (2006). *Mindset: The new psychology of success.* New York, NY: Random House.

Earl, L. (2003). *Assessment as learning: Using classroom assessment to maximize student learning.* Thousand Oaks, CA: Corwin.

Frey, N., Fisher, D., & Everlove, S. (2009). *Productive group work: How to engage students, build teamwork, and promote understanding.* Alexandria, VA: Association for Supervision and Curriculum Development.

Gardner, H. (2006). *Multiple intelligences: New horizons in theory and practice.* New York, NY: Basic Books.

Geake, J. G. (2009). *The brain at school: Educational neuroscience in the classroom.* New York, NY: McGraw-Hill.

Goleman, D. (2006). Teaching to student strengths: The socially intelligent leader. *Educational Leadership, 64*(1), 76–81.

Gregory, G. H., & Kaufeldt, M. (2012). *Think big, start small: How to differentiate instruction in a brain friendly classroom.* Bloomington, IN: Solution Tree Press.

Gurian, M., Henley, P., & Trueman, T. (2001). *Boys and girls learn differently: A guide for teachers and parents.* San Francisco, CA: Jossey-Bass.

Gurian, M., & Stevens, K. (2005). *The minds of boys: Saving our sons from falling behind in school and life.* San Francisco, CA: Jossey–Bass.

Hallowell, E. M. (2011). *Shine: Using brain science to get the best from your people.* Boston, MA. Harvard Business School.

Healy, J. (2010). *Different learners: Identifying, preventing, and treating your child's learning problems.* New York, NY: Simon & Schuster.

Immordino-Yang, M. H., & Damasio, A. (2007). We feel, therefore we learn: The relevance of affective and social neuroscience to education. *Mind, Brain, and Education, 1*(1), 3–10.

Johnson, D. W., & Johnson, F. P. (2009). *Joining together* (10th ed.). Upper Saddle River, NJ: Pearson.

Marzano, R. J. (2007). *The art and science of teaching: A comprehensive framework for effective instruction.* Alexandria, VA: Association for Supervision and Curriculum Development.

Marzano, R. J., & Brown, J. L. (2009). *A handbook for the art and science of teaching.* Alexandria, VA: Association for Supervision and Curriculum Development.

National Council for Accreditation of Teacher Education. (2010). *The road less travelled: How the developmental sciences can prepare educators to improve student achievement: Policy recommendations.* Washington, DC: Author.

Panksepp, J. (1998). *Affective neuroscience: The foundations of human and animal emotions.* New York, NY: Oxford University Press.

Ratey, J. J. (2008). *Spark: The revolutionary new science of exercise and the brain.* New York, NY: Little, Brown.

Reeves, D. (2000). Standards are not enough: Essential transformations for school success. *NASSP Bulletin, 84,* 5–19.

Sax, L. (2005). *Why gender matters.* New York, NY: Doubleday.

Silver, H. F., & Perrini, M. (2010). The 8 C's of engagement: How learning styles and instructional design increase student commitment to learning. In R. Marzano (Ed.), *On excellence in teaching* (pp. 319–344). Bloomington, IN: Solution Tree Press.

Sousa, D. A. (2006). *How the brain learns* (3rd ed.). Thousand Oaks, CA: Corwin.

Sousa, D. A. (Ed.). (2010). *Mind, brain, and education: Neuroscience implications for the classroom.* Bloomington, IN: Solution Tree Press.

Sousa, D. A. (2011). *What principals need to know about the basics of creating brain-compatible classrooms.* Bloomington, IN: Solution Tree Press.

Sousa, D. A., & Tomlinson, C. A. (2010). *Differentiation and the brain: How neuroscience supports the learner-friendly classroom.* Bloomington, IN: Solution Tree Press.

Stiggins, R. J. (2001). *Student-involved classroom assessment* (3rd ed.). Upper Saddle River, NJ: Merrill Prentice Hall.

Vygotsky, L. S. (1978). *Mind in society: The development of higher psychological processes.* Cambridge, MA: Harvard University Press.

Willis, J. (2010). Want children to "pay attention"? Make their brains curious! *Psychology Today.* Retrieved from http://www.psychologytoday.com/blog/radical-teaching/201005/want-children-pay-attention-make-their-brains-curious

Zull, J. (2002). *The art of changing the brain.* Sterling, VA: Stylus.

Index

CORWIN

A SAGE Company

The Corwin logo—a raven striding across an open book—represents the union of courage and learning. Corwin is committed to improving education for all learners by publishing books and other professional development resources for those serving the field of PreK–12 education. By providing practical, hands-on materials, Corwin continues to carry out the promise of its motto: **"Helping Educators Do Their Work Better."**

CPSIA information can be obtained
at www.ICGtesting.com
Printed in the USA
BVHW060833070522
636380BV00002B/3